CW00428224

www.united-pc.eu

Bedbugs, Blisters and Brain Surgery

The true story of a teenager who survived 2 bouts of neurosurgery to walk the historic 500 mile, Camino de Santiago

by
Martin Moorman

Preface

All profits from sales of this book will go to BTRS (Brain Tumour Research Trust) who support the work of the Neurosurgery team based at Leeds General Infirmary in the UK, to find a lasting cure to brain related trauma.

Life... and the way we choose to do it is weird. It sometimes defies logic.

My decision to write the forward to this book on a wet Halifax morning on Saturday 24 March 2018 at 08.45 has no real logic.

Why write it now?

The answer lies somewhere in the timing; the neat passage of time where the most intense personal journey for my family, over a four year period, has reached its natural conclusion. It is a now happy conclusion, something which hopefully makes this book a better and more enjoyable experience for the reader. Whilst the conclusion is a happy one, the journey to reach it was torturous, painful and at times emotional.

It really did hurt.

I guess the answer also lies in the fact that with the first anniversary of the most exciting journey I have ever undertaken, fast approaching in just 5 days' time, I have been completely re-motivated to pick up my pen and start to seriously edit and finalise the contents of this book.

I've never written a book before. I've had plenty of articles published through my job as a teacher in a special school, but never a book. If 3 years ago you had predicted that I would become an author recounting a most incredible personal journey, I would have laughed!

So, I hope you enjoy this read and that in some small way, the story of Jake and his amazing recovery from 2 harrowing bouts of brain surgery through to the completion of a 500 mile walk along a historic medieval pilgrimage route, will inspire, motivate and perhaps reassure you that however the dark circumstances appear, there is always hope.

I hope it will especially reassure the reader who is perhaps facing life threatening or changing circumstances themselves. I repeat; the biggest reassurance I can offer and one I believe Jake's story is testament to, is that there is always hope!

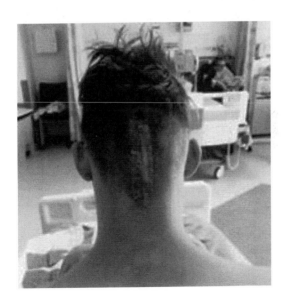

Foreword

by

Jake Moorman

When Dad asked me to write the foreword to his book my instant reaction was to say a resounding yes. It is only now that I actually begin to write that I realise my ignorance, as I am not entirely sure what a foreword should entail. Nevertheless, I will attempt to provide a sufficient introduction for this story.

Whilst it could be argued that a large proportion of this book revolves around my story, I personally would never consider this story to be my own. It was without doubt our story and it affected the lives of each member of our family very differently.

I cannot think of anyone more suited to commit this extraordinary journey to paper the than my dad. I think the combination of having been an observer to what happened whilst still being intimately involved and affected gives dad a unique perspective from which to write this book. I have found his perspective to be incredibly honest and refreshing and, whilst I might be slightly biased, I truly believe this story will have a positive impact on anyone and everyone who reads it.

My dad and I have always been close. Our whole family has. I think my two older siblings, Harry and Rosie, would agree when I say I think we have the greatest parents in the world. When I look back over my 20 years of life, I have a wealth of truly beautiful memories for which I know I am extremely blessed and fortunate. Of all of these memories there are very few where Dad was not involved.

The contents of this book will enable the reader to focus on a four year time scale in my life. Whilst a relatively short period, it was a time that had a massive impact. It is important for you (the reader) to be aware that, as is the case with every story, our lives were happening long before this book was ever conceived or written and, they will hopefully continue long after its publication.

If I have learnt anything from the journey of the last 4 years, it is that life matters. Not just in the grand sense, but within ordinary, day-to-day occurrences, life still matters.

There were numerous times during this story where I think we all wished things would just be normal again. This has taught me to really try to appreciate life especially in times of routine and normality. This story was certainly conceived at a time when things for our family were far from normal, and uncertainty was running rampant in each of our lives.

As you might have guessed by the fact that I am writing this foreword, this story has a happy ending, but that doesn't change the fact that these were some of the darkest times that dad, myself and our family ever faced.

One of my dad's most distinguishing characteristics is his almost eternal optimism (unless football-related). I think this book reflects that outlook and is an example of just how to make the best of a bad situation.

I will conclude by simply reiterating how proud I am of my dad for his dedication to telling this story truthfully and for his unrelenting desire to attempt to bring some positivity into the lives of other people. I am inspired by my dad on a daily basis and think if we can all be more like him the world would be a better place.

Jacob Moorman; Tuesday 3rd January 2019, Whitby, UK

This book is dedicated to 3 parties:

First, to the neurosurgical team based at Leeds General Infirmary in Northern England and especially Paul, Neurosurgeon and Dominic, Senior Anaesthetist in the Leeds Teaching Hospitals Trust. Their medical expertise transformed a situation where Jake lay on his deathbed and was told; 'you could die on the ward,' into a life full of opportunities and purpose. They are remarkably skilled and professional medics as well as 2 of the best people I have ever met.

Second, to a remarkable young man, my son Jake, who showed immense resilience, steadfastness, faith and courage within the most frightening of experiences. His Mum (my wife Nicky) Rosie and Harry his sister and brother and the many family members and friends who unstintingly backed him and us, especially when the chips were really down.

Finally, but most importantly, to a miracle working God who answered our prayers (and those of our numerous supporters, known and unknown) and pulled Jake out of those 'rough waters' on 2 separate occasions and blessed him with the most exciting of futures.

I would like to thank the following companies for their kit sponsorship for our Camino de Santiago walk of 2017: Vango UK, Petzl, Helly Hansen and especially Geoff and the team at BAC Elland, our local outdoor gear shop, who were so supportive and encouraging.

Isaiah 43 vs 1-5 *(The Message Translation)*

But now, God's Message, the God who made you in the first place, Jacob, the One who got you started, Israel: "Don't be afraid, I've redeemed you. I've called your name. You're mine. When you're in over your head, I'll be there with you. When you're in rough waters, you will not go down. When you're between a rock and a hard place, it won't be a dead end – because I am God, your personal God, The Holy of Israel, your Saviour. I paid a huge price for you: all of Egypt, with rich Cush and Seba thrown in! That's how much you mean to me! That's how much I love you! I's sell the whole world to get you back, trade the creation just for you. So, don't be afraid: I'm with you."

Part One

'The type of news you never want to hear'

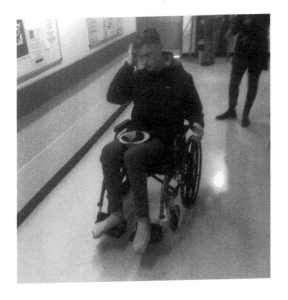

Chapter One

'Every parent's worst nightmare'

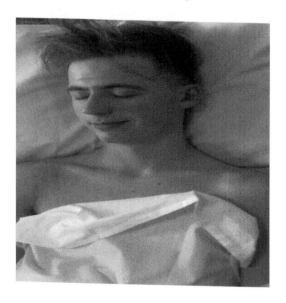

We've all heard the saying 'every parent's worst nightmare' and I guess most parents have used it. For me, the phrase became all too real on 5th April 2014. That was the defining moment, the day when our world as parents and as a family almost caved in. That was the date my youngest son Jake, aged just 15, was diagnosed as having a 2 cm bleed on the brain.

Nothing prepared me for that news. It was, for my wife Nicky and I, our worst possible nightmare.

Looking back, it should have been perhaps more obvious than I realized at the time. Jake had been unwell for the preceding 8 weeks. His illness had started whilst he was on a family break with Harry, Nicky and I. We had flown to Lanzarote for a week of winter sun during February half term 2014. Whilst we enjoyed a fabulous break Jake was periodically sick and complained of occasional headaches; naturally we had dismissed this as a 'holiday tummy bug'.

During that week and the following weeks once he was back in school for the remainder of the spring term, Jake continued to suffer from irregular bouts of vomiting and headaches. There was no pattern, they would come and go. We presumed, just as most parents would, that he still had a virus that would clear over time. We took him to see the GP on several occasions. They carried out all the neurological tests, that 2 years later we would develop a depressing familiarity with. They could find nothing wrong.

To my eternal chagrin, I still recollect the morning on a cold and dark school day in March 2014 where I once again had to coerce Jake out of bed. I was under time pressure myself as I was late for school. (I'm the Headteacher of a secondary special school in Halifax.)

I'm still ashamed to admit my empathy levels weren't where they should be. He was suffering with another headache and my exasperated response to him as he lay there moaning was for him to 'man up.' My reasoning was simple, if somewhat unsympathetic; we all struggle on those dark, cold winter mornings; he felt ill, I feel ill occasionally. We just have to get on with it.

I literally had to drag him out of bed and to the bus stop. The next day of course he would seem less out of sorts. There really was no pattern. So, when that phone call came from Nicky, on 5th April 2014, I was completely floored. I had never considered the thought of brain haemorrhage. It sounded serious, scary, an unseen and brooding menace and I felt an impending sense of doom!

Chapter Two

'Stuck on repeat'

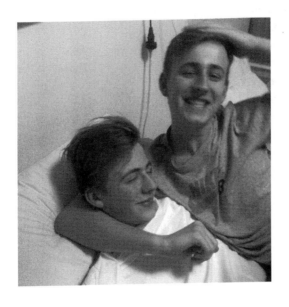

When you see a Doctor and get a diagnosis, the temptation is to always believe that you will then immediately crack on with your treatment and recovery. That is what I expected for Jake once his diagnosis was made. What I didn't expect was that he would then proceed to spend the next 4 weeks either at home (although never for very long) or more likely either at the Calderdale Royal Hospital, Halifax, or on increasingly regular occasions, 20 miles away at the Leeds General Infirmary.

It soon became clear, in Jake's case at least, that there were no easy answers and that the most appropriate medical treatment was to manage without surgical intervention. The medical team consistently sought to 'conservatively manage' the issue and this became our experience from the outset.

The doctors explained that the bleed was in such a complex and 'hard to reach' area of Jake's brain, that it was always going to be a last resort for them to operate. The bleed was deep into his brain, near the fourth ventricle, in the cerebellum.

The fourth ventricle, we were told, allows the fluid that surrounds and protects the brain to drain away. Getting to it via surgery was highly risky. They warned us that they didn't even know what had caused the bleed or the origin as the MRI and CT scans were obscured by old blood which hid the precise site of the fresher bleed.

We had a pretty simple message to digest from day one; we needed to wait and wait… and wait.

The doctors explained that there was a hope that as the bleed stopped, the blood would be reabsorbed and future scans would show just where the bleed was located and what was causing it, thus giving a plan of action. Meanwhile the best treatment, unless he worsened, was for us all to wait.

So, our lives had a frustrating predictability about them. On the days when Jake was feeling better, we would dare to believe that maybe things would just clear up naturally. But as often as he had a decent day, the reality was that he frequently experienced dreadful days where the headaches were blindingly painful. He would persistently vomit whenever he smelt food or drink, let alone taste it, as the bleed was putting pressure on and thus stimulating the vomit centre in his brain. He started to dehydrate and lose a worrying amount of weight. As a very tall and skinny teenager, he didn't have a lot of weight that he could afford to lose.

The days blended into weeks and we became more and more resigned to a seemingly never-ending nightmare.

Chapter Three

'The longest day'

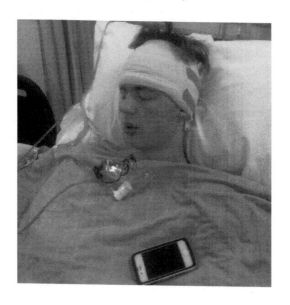

It became apparent during the latter part of April 2014, that Jake was not getting any better. In fact, he was starting to become more and more physically sick and the medical team were increasingly worried that his persistent retching and nausea was causing a further strain and pressure at the bleed point deep in his cerebellum and that there was the real potential for further bleeds, in that most vulnerable area of the brain. They warned that hydrocephalus was a very stark possibility and that they would have no options but to operate if that was the case. Hydrocephalus can arise when internal pressure builds on the brain and is dangerous.

So, it transpired that we received the news that we didn't ever want to hear on the evening of 30th April 2014; "Jake is developing hydrocephalus and there is a real chance he will die on the ward if we don't operate as soon as possible. Jake will be the first into theatre tomorrow morning."

It is a very sobering moment for any parent when their son aged just 16, is asked to consent to brain surgery.

Jake had turned 16 just 8 days earlier and therefore in the UK, he was acknowledged to have capacity to give his own surgical consent. The risk list was long and agonizing to hear: death, paralysis, mutism, becoming wheelchair bound. The odds of complications were identified as 12%; great odds of success in the more normal context of an exam or on a football pitch, but much more daunting when facing brain surgery. Additionally, we were warned that his planned surgery the next day, was 'unique and complicated.'

The following 24 hours really were to prove the longest day ever for our family.

Remarkably within all the turmoil that this change of circumstances had created, there was one person who appeared to stay calm and resolute throughout; Jake. I emphasise the word 'appeared.' We all know that appearances can be very deceptive! Much later in 2018, Jake actually confided to me that throughout this time, he was in complete turmoil internally. His faith in his own survival, let alone recovery was sorely tested and doubt was his primary influence.

This revelation from Jake in 2018 really challenged me. I guess it reaffirmed to me just how human beings can 'present a front' where we appear to be able to cope; in fact, we often can't and don't. I experienced that myself in late 2017 as I tried to come to terms with the sudden death of my sister Anna. Professionally, I put on a mask, and tried to hide what had happened. Physically I was in work, but mentally I was in another place, a very messed up place. It took 2 weeks before I eventually opened up and told the staff in school of my loss. Being open and transparent and therefore completely vulnerable, within our darkest moments is often so hard.

Looking back with a more emotionally detached perspective, I believe there were other reasons why Jake seemed calm and resolute.

On a more practical level, Jake had felt ill for months, been very ill for at least 10 weeks and seriously sick for at least 7 of them. He was exhausted from the persistent vomiting and emaciated. I suspected that he had started to view his quality of life as having diminished to a perpetual state of abject misery. Surgery would give him hope at the very least, hope that there could be a return to a normal teenage life, hope that he could return to skateboarding and hanging out with his friends. The alternative of staying in hospital, for weeks and months into the future with no change, really gave him no future. Additionally, Jake seemed convicted that this treatment would be successful and that it was necessary to go through the surgery to get the result he wanted. Later, he told me that it was only his Mum's deep faith and conviction that he would pull through surgery, that had sustained him in the build-up to this first operation. His own admission, expressed to me in 2018, was that back in 2014 his own level of faith was at an all-time low.

Some readers might consider the concept of faith to be blind optimism within the darkest of circumstances, but for Jake his Mum's strong Christian faith gave him something to cling to and a hope that things would work out well.

For his Mum and Dad, publicly at least there was a degree of certainty and trust that 'God had him'. Inside though I too was truly was in bits. I really felt like I was going to lose my son. But I knew that I couldn't ever express that fear publicly, for the crushing effect in could have for all of our family and besides, I knew that we had no other non-surgical options.

So, on 1 May 2014 in the small preparation room off the operating theatre in Leeds General Infirmary at 8:45 am Nicky and I hugged Jake and said goodbye. It was a tearful moment; one that I desperately tried to camouflage with a jovial British 'stiff upper lip' response whilst my inner fear that he would not survive the surgery was very real.

Nicky and I left the hospital to wander the streets of Leeds aimlessly for 7 long hours. The only time we made any meaningful decisions in those subsequent hours was when through necessity, I bought a new green 'V' necked jumper. The necessity was provided by Nicky who had 'borrowed' my coat on that day as hers was at home. Leeds was freezing cold on 1 May 2014 and I had to buy something to at least try to keep myself warm and stop my persistent shivering. To be fair it was a pretty smart 'designer' jumper; a change from my usual sportswear attire and it only cost me £15 in the sale, so a real bargain in my eyes. I still own it and wear it even now; I intentionally wear it every year on the anniversary of that operation, as a physical acknowledgement of the miraculous transformation in Jake's life, it remains one of my favourite jumpers, especially as it holds such momentous significance.

Over the subsequent hours we ate nothing, we just kept on moving around central Leeds. Incredibly Dominic, the anaesthetist, stayed true to his word and rang us on the dot very 2 hours to provide us with a cheery and reassuring update on Jake's progress. In the third phone update he asked how we were coping and if we'd eaten; when we said we felt too sick to eat he asked if I was a cyclist? A strange question but I answered in the affirmative, I have always cycled to and from work in over 30 years of teaching. "In that case he said, you will be familiar with Rule Number 5 of the 'Velominati'.

"I have no idea what you are talking about" I said. Dominic's reply was a recommendation for me to look up its meaning.

Miraculously Jake came through his operation.

At about 7 pm that evening, as he lay groaning with acute pain in the postoperative recovery room after more than 7 hours of complicated neurosurgery, Jake struggled to focus his gaze on me as I sat beside him in my new green V neck trying to soothe him with comforting words and my hand mopping his brow. He struggled to form his first post-surgery words; "You look gay"! I have never relished an un-PC observation so much. In that simple three-word sentence, my son had confirmed that he was alive, he could identify and talk to us and I started to believe that we could dare to hope that he would now fully recover. Even now, four years on, I can't condone his stereotyping or use of inappropriate terminology or language but how I loved the unspoken message that those three words conveyed.

That night, as I sat at his bedside. I kept drifting off to sleep, only to be woken by Jake who was in great discomfort and wanted to be moved or repositioned as he lay in bed. He was connected to all sorts of monitors and machines with a central venous line in his neck, so he really did need my help. I was a rubbish nurse that night. I guess the reality of my relief that he had survived surgery, allowed me to sleep well, in between Jake's frequent awakenings, for the first time in weeks.

I remember deciding to 'Google' the suggestion made by Dominic about 'Velominati, Rule Number 5.' Just before I fell asleep, I remember reading the Google description and giggling to myself as I read and re-read the meaning:

'Harden the f*** up!'

Chapter Four

'The long and winding road'

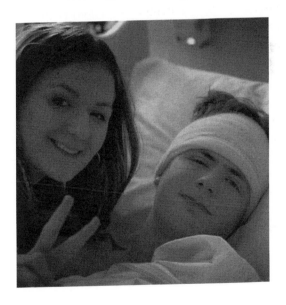

In the immediate aftermath of Jake's operation, it became apparent that very little had actually changed; apart from him having undergone and survived highly technical and complicated brain surgery.

Jake remained sick, very sick.

His vomiting continued and the blinding headaches that accompanied it still plagued him. He needed help in every aspect of his care: to get out of bed, to get to the toilet, to drink a spoonful of soup; which he would then immediately bring back up. Immediately after surgery his day to day quality of life could not really be claimed to have improved in any way. He really was very, very sick and he had lost an alarming amount of weight.

It was at least 5 days after surgery, before a tiny change for the better was evident. He started to play some chess and Nicky and I dared to borrow a wheelchair for him and escape the hospital. We ventured out for a half mile trip into Leeds City Centre. It was another freezing cold day and Jake was very cold, but it was a milestone, his first trip out of hospital for weeks. That slow improvement developed over the next days and it meant that 9 days after his operation, Jake was allowed to come home. Still very sick and still under close medical scrutiny, he was at last, beginning to digest some fluids and to actually take an interest in life.

As we became more confident in his ability to cope, we dared to venture a little further afield, even reaching the

'White Rose' Shopping Centre on the outskirts of Leeds on one occasion to look for a suit for his upcoming school prom. I remember him complaining at my wheelchair pushing technique on that particular trip. In return for all the complaints, I took my revenge and parked him in the corner of a shop with his wheelchair brakes on and walked off leaving him totally marooned for a couple of minutes. Jake claims not to remember this joke, preferring to focus on an alleged incident where I allegedly rammed him into a shelf of iPod docking stations in another shop. I quite understandably, have no recollection of this incident! The wheelchair parking incident was all in jest of course. Soft hearted as I am, I returned for him within a minute.

The family banter that we all enjoy, on a daily basis was beginning to return after an absence of many months. Unfortunately, Jake was unable to sit his GCSE examinations in May 2014. He was still very ill. He spent most of June and early July 2014 continuing with his very gradual recovery.

When the first 2 stages of the Tour de France International cycling race came to Yorkshire in early July 2014 Jake was at last well enough to actually enjoy the event as a spectator and watch it with his family at the bottom of our hill. We witnessed some of the world's most elite cyclists, including Mark Cavendish and Chris Froome zipping past us in a blur. We were joined for the weekend by many of our closest family members as we sought to celebrate his recovery as well as his brother

Harry's 18th birthday. We watched the local part of the Halifax-based stage in our immediate neighbourhood, just 800 metres from our front door.

It seemed so ironic that after nearly 6 long months of illness, worry and anguish that such a momentous world sporting event should be experienced in just 2 minutes 13 seconds. We had waited on that street corner for over 4 hours to witness this event of local and regional significance that actually lasted just over 2 minutes! I remember reflecting once again, on that irony as we watched the peloton of riders' speed past us at the bottom of the hill from our house.

Chapter Five

'Every pilgrim has a reason'

During the long days that followed his surgery in May 2014, Jake still had significant bouts of inactivity. Initially he based himself in our bed, but after 2 weeks, despite being very weak and wobbly and very thin from weight loss, he came downstairs during the day.

Nicky and I shared his care, I still went to work whilst she took time off from her job for the full summer term. Leading staff and Governors at both of the schools we worked at were very supportive.

This meant that there were times when I would leave work early and I could be with Jake whilst Nicky took some time out. He wasn't well enough to do many things; board games exhausted him, and he couldn't easily concentrate on books. As a result, in the main, we watched lots of films and box sets: we loved Band of Brothers, Hatfields and McCoys and Prison Break. We were roundly criticized by his Mum and Grandma for watching these "violent films". To be fair they really were quite tame, compared to many other TV dramas we could have watched.

We loved them. We loved the shared experience.

Then one day, he told me about 'The Way' starring Martin Sheen. I had never heard of it, it still surprises me that so many people still haven't heard of it. By default, I'm even more surprised that so many people, in the UK in particular, still haven't heard of the Camino de Santiago. We watched 'The Way' together, after just 10 minutes, my eyes caught his and we both nodded. That night, we determined that we too would walk the Camino de Santiago.

Chapter Six

'Return to normality'

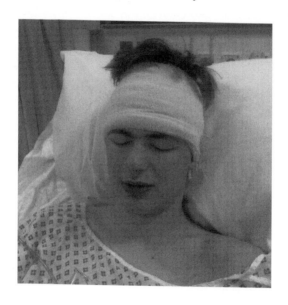

As the summer of 2014 progressed so Jake gradually recovered his health. It took a long time.

The celebration of The Tour de France coming to Halifax, held a triple significance for us. It took place at the time to celebrate his brother Harry's 18th birthday and it also coincided with Jake's apparent recovery to full health; it gave us the opportunity to celebrate both of these with our family.

Even now when we watch a link to the Tour de France bike race from any year and in any country (the first 2 stages of 'Le Tour' are always ridden in another European country) my mind drifts back to that most special of weekends, where many of our nearest and dearest family members travelled from all over the UK to Halifax, to celebrate with us.

Just like in those surreal memories of childhood we all seem to remember, on that weekend the sun shone beautifully. On the day before the race itself the boys in the family invaded a local Tour de France inspired Beer Festival, just 1 mile up the road where we sampled the full range of guest beers. We saw yellow painted bikes adorn most of the houses and gardens on the entire route of the bike race. It really was a Tour de France 'Takeover Weekend.'

A local curfew of motorized vehicles on the 'Tour route' on the day of the race, meant that everyone walked to their personal race vantage point, meaning that whole families became absorbed into the event; it really did have a special community feel that I have yet to see matched anywhere since. It felt positive, vibrant, yellow... just like Jake's future. Despite his inability to sit his GCSE exams Jake was still able to accrue 5 A-C passes in total. He had, prior to becoming ill, been identified as a 'straight A student' in all 12 subjects studied.

My sense of helplessness in being unable to overcome his medical condition, was replaced with an anger at an education system that in my view had badly let my son down and had denied him the qualifications that he had worked so hard for during his previous school years. It felt so unfair! It wasn't his fault that he had been too sick to sit his final exams. I felt a profound sense of injustice on his behalf. The authorities had made no allowances for the fact that in his 2 years of GCSE study he had consistently secured A and A* grades in all areas. His inability to sit a final exam, meant that he was denied the certification that I believe he was entitled too.

I railed against the Chief Executive of OFQUAL, (The Office of Qualifications and Examinations Regulation) or the flawed system that let my son down. I thundered my anger through countless letters to Michael Gove, then UK Education Secretary, whose recommendation to return to a linear exam system in my mind, prevented Jake from securing his rightful results.

Despite my protestations Jake was awarded just 5 GCSE's.

Protesting vehemently at least made me feel better!

We received great support with our appeal from Jake's school and fortunately they showed much greater flexibility than The Department of Education, admitting him to the Sixth Form to study 4-A level subjects. This was despite him not achieving their prescribed entry criteria of 6 GCSE's minimum.

I eventually dropped my frustrations at his academic treatment. Four years on, he is successfully studying Geology and Geography at The University of Leeds. Those missing GCSE qualifications have been replaced by higher level results. Jake started his A-Level studies in September 2014, successfully sat his Mathematics GCSE in autumn 2014 and so secured his 6th GCSE. He proceeded to start to enjoy school and life again.

Paul, his neurosurgeon was always candid though. He consistently told us that he still had no medical reason for the cause of the brain haemorrhages Jake had suffered. They had removed 'something' during surgery, but he was honest enough with us, to confirm that they hadn't been able to positively identify what. With that uncertainty he could give us no assurances for Jake's future, but he did tell Jake to 'Go and get on with your life.' He even supported a return to skateboarding.

The only thing Paul told Jake to do was to avoid flying abroad.

Normality had seemed to return, and Jake embraced it.

Chapter Seven

'Winging it'

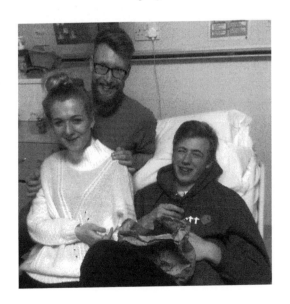

Jake's progress was good throughout the remainder of 2014 and into Spring 2015. We began to dare that he had indeed made a full recovery. The medics kept a close eye on him. It was only after a consultation in Spring 2015 that we realised there was still a problem. As ever with such news, there was a good and a bad side to it.

The good news was that his consultant was now pretty sure what was causing the problem. The bad news was that the only way to deal with it, was through surgery.

The facts and the nature of the new haemorrhage were explained to us all. The spotlight was on Jake to decide if and when to have surgery. His response was unprecedented and remarkable. He looked Paul straight in the eye and said:

"Can we wing it?"

Jake's reasoning was simple but quite understandable. Whilst another bleed had been confirmed, he was actually feeling much better, his final A-level exams were less than a year away and if his neurosurgeon was correct and his health allowed it, Jake could postpone surgery till after he had sat his exams and elect for it in summer 2016 when all academic milestones would have been reached. He had been cheated of achieving the qualifications he deserved in 2014, he naturally wanted to try and avoid that situation re-occurring in 2016. His neurosurgeon accepted Jake's request. He told him that in his own personal view, Jake would need surgery at some point, but agreed, that if 'winging it' allowed Jake to sit those exams, then he would be happy to support him.

Once again in the later part of 2015 a second period of 'conservative management' began; this time at the instigation of Jake.

Chapter Eight

'Edinburgh and three men named Jimmy'

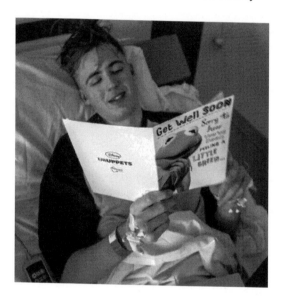

On 27th December 2015, with the full endorsement of the medical team, Jake, his Mum, Dad and brother Harry joined our longstanding family friends the Hughes' for our annual New Year week family holiday.

This time we headed to a small peninsula south of Newton Stewart, about 10 miles east of Stranraer on the West Scottish coast. We were due to stay in a self-catering cottage overlooking the Atlantic. It looked fantastic and we were all very excited. After a long 6 hour drive from Halifax we arrived at our coastal cottage at tea time on the Saturday evening. Jake was straight out of the car and headed off on his skateboard in the rapidly diminishing daylight of the late afternoon whilst I unloaded our gear. All was well. We were looking forward to another fantastic break with our best friends.

The following morning, just as his Mum was lacing her boots for our first family walk, Jake was violently sick. The symptoms were obvious. He and we knew the signs and recognized the implications. We rang the staff on the neurology ward at Leeds General Infirmary. Their response was unequivocal; an ambulance journey with full 'blues and twos' 70 miles down the coast to Dumfries.

Over the next week he stayed 3 days in Dumfries hospital, 3 days in Edinburgh Infirmary and 1 day in Leeds General Infirmary. On each occasion he was transported by ambulance with the full siren treatment and paramedic support. In total Jake and his Mum travelled more than 600 miles in these ambulance journeys. She never left him.

Those 3 days in Edinburgh fell across New Year's Eve on a ward that contained just 3 other patients; bizarrely all called Jimmy. Nicky stayed with him, sleeping in a visitor's room, located by a kindly nurse. She had arrived in Edinburgh wearing just the clothes she was in, without any money or access to it. I was stuck 150 miles away in Newton Stewart with Harry and our friends. The nursing team on the neurological ward in Edinburgh rallied round; they fed her, provided a bed and supplied her with some money to buy a change of clean underwear and a toothbrush… yet another random act of kindness by people we will never meet again; kindness that we will never forget.

On the evening of 31st December, the 3 Jimmy's, Nicky and Jake watched the world-famous Edinburgh New Year fireworks display from the hospital ward window. Two days later he was back in Leeds General Infirmary, meeting with Paul his neurosurgeon who offered him an imminent date for surgery later in January 2016.

He was told that 'winging it' was no longer an option, and so, my world, or I should say our world, turned upside down for the second time in 2 years.

I honestly felt that having cheated death the first time, Jake was not going to get a second reprieve. I truly felt that this time around I would surely lose my son.

Chapter Nine

'Been here before'

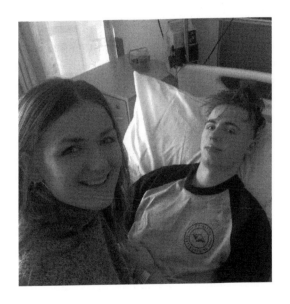

On 9th of February 2016 Jake underwent complex neurosurgery for the second time. The journey leading up to the day of surgery was difficult and fraught with uncertainty.

His first scheduled date for surgery in late January 2016 had been cancelled at the last minute due to industrial action by junior doctors across the UK. As it turned out this cancellation proved to be a blessing in disguise. Jake was actually very poorly throughout January meaning that his recovery from surgery would have been potentially more challenging.

On the day of actual surgery, a shortage of beds on the High Dependency ward meant that he was once again facing a cancellation. He was actually dressed for surgery at this time and emotionally prepared for it, so the 'disappointment' on his face was all the more tangible and upsetting.

Just as we started to accept that it would not be this day, a bed was miraculously released at 11:00. This was at precisely the same time that 'LEAD' - a leadership conference based at our church in Bradford involving church leaders representing over 500 churches across the UK - was interrupted and his traumatic situation became a focus for the prayers of those 500 church leaders. It seemed to us that with Jake, every time his plight became desperate, he seemed to receive a divine and miraculous intervention.

Jake began neurosurgery for the second time at 11:45 on 9th February 2016 and for us, this became our longest ever day.

However, within all the worry and concern, this time we were wiser and more intentional. We didn't aimlessly walk the streets of Leeds, but instead drove the 9 miles to Bradford and attended that same Leadership Conference. To be amongst people with a strong faith, at precisely the time where our faith was being severely tested, was a true blessing. I can remember little detail of that afternoon's seminars, but I remember thinking that I wouldn't actually want to be anywhere else. The power that we felt in that room on that day was indescribable. I somehow knew that everything was going to be fine.

A long 11 hours after his second bout of surgery started, we visited Jake in the Recovery Room just off the operating theatre.

His pain and discomfort were obvious and very upsetting to us as parents. His words were slurred and unintelligible, but despite his cries of pain, once again I could offer up my thanks: he was alive, he recognised us, and he could make sounds. Speech would come later. But for now, I was just overjoyed that Jake was alive.

Chapter Ten

'A setback can be a set up'

Around the time of this second bout of surgery I can remember hearing a 'talk' at my church about 'a setback being a setup'. The fact that the speaker was one of the best; a young guy called Dave who leads Life Church in Leeds with his wife, is only part of the reason I remember it so well.

His biblical text was the story of Joseph. His point? Every time Joseph received a perceived set back, it proved to be a set up to something significantly better.

In his teaching Dave emphasized the inevitability that we all face setbacks in our lives, but that if we trust God, just like Joseph, we would often find that these setbacks could prove be a setup. So, it was with Jake and his second bout of neurosurgery.

I would never have imagined that at the end of his 2 long years of serious illness, Jake and I would be set up for a better than ever father/son experience, that would bind us closer than ever before in a never to be forgotten way. The experience would also involve Jake's brother, a cousin he only sees intermittently, his Mum, sister and an Auntie living in France, alongside hundreds of supporters and well-wishers. I could never have imagined that we would both undertake a challenge that neither of us had even heard of just 2 years before. I still marvel that this challenge would involve us walking 500 miles across Spain, just 1 year after major brain surgery.

I am still flabbergasted that we would be able to mutually find the necessary fitness and time of at least 30 days to try to achieve it.

But we did.

Miraculously we were setup to take on the iconic and historical Camino de Santiago in April 2017. On Thursday 30 March 2017, some 13 months after surviving his second and much longer operation, Jake, Harry and I flew from Stansted Airport to Biarritz in South Western France; the gateway to St Jean Pied de Port, the official starting point to the Camino Frances.

We hugged Nicky goodbye in Stansted short stay car park at and proceeded through check in, to board our plane to Biarritz. Our worldly possessions for the next 32 days were packed into three small rucksacks. With Camino Pilgrim shells attached to our bags we were about to embark on the most exciting of adventures.

We were so excited and so very grateful.

Part Two

'El Camino de Santiago - The Camino Frances'

Introduction

Thursday 30th March 2017
'The French Connection: A rendezvous in Biarritz'

Our flight was normal. It was on time and there were no budget airline moments. We disembarked on the tarmac at the small provincial airport in Biarritz and proceeded to the queue through French security and border checks.

As we waited in the glass access tunnel that led to the security desk my younger sister Lizzie with my nephew Daniel were clearly visible some 20 metres away, holding their 'Moorman Boys do the Way' welcome banner. It was hot and stuffy and took us over an hour to negotiate that particular piece of French bureaucracy.

Liz had travelled 5 hours from her home near Albi, north east of Toulouse to collect us and drive us up to the official start village of the Camino Frances, St John Pied de Port, situated about 60 kilometres from Biarritz, high up in the French Pyrenees.

We located a Pilgrim hostel relatively easily and were checked in by an Australian 'Hospitallero' (volunteer) named Bryson, who we would meet again some 30 days later in Santiago. He had a unique personality, was profoundly deaf and with a strong lisp. Bryson was funny, a larger than life character and a brilliant lip reader who was very patient and nurturing of my clumsy and rather amateur use of British Sign Language. He was an Aston Villa FC supporter... well someone has to be!

The 4 English boys (Dan claims to be Welsh but was actually born in Trowbridge) shared a dormitory room with Lizzie and a French speaking Canadian lady who was moved by Jakes story and our reason for walking the Camino. It soon became apparent that Jake would need to repeat his story with increasingly regularity over the next month. We chatted to Tony from London, at a crossroads in his career and walking the Camino to muse over his options taking some time out of normal life. We learnt then that most Pilgrims have a 'reason for walking'.

We quickly learned that on Camino, you have to adapt. As it was Sunday evening, Lizzie had brought meat balls and pasta for our supper knowing the shops would be closed. However, our forethought was of little use as the hostel had no means to heat the food! We resorted to pizza and beer from a local takeaway. Admittedly this was not the ideal pre-Camino meal for finely tuned athletes, but we didn't care, it was delicious!

That night, I slept badly. This was probably due to a mixture of excitement and the fact that I hadn't felt particularly well for the preceding 2 weeks prior to flying out to France. Whilst my fellow pilgrims snored, I found myself shivering and sweating in equal measures throughout the night. Consequently, I was awake at 5 am and learnt another valuable lesson in planning before and during a Camino, when I found that the toilet had no paper!

DISTANCE TRAVELLED: 0 km
DISTANCE TO SANTIAGO: 799 km

Chapter One

Friday 31st March 2017
Camino Day One: St Jean Pied de Port to Burguete

We set off at 7:30 am as daylight started to pierce the pretty village of St Jean. We were boosted and buoyed by Lizzie's enthusiastic farewell, she had supplied breakfast which was devoured at speed, the only limitation on that morning was the space around that breakfast table as all our fellow pilgrims were also trying to get up and out for a speedy exit. We had a 6 hour hike up and over the Pyrenees ahead of us with a minimum distance of 27 kilometres to walk. Our time and daylight were very precious. We wanted to crack on!

Lizzie had a five hour drive back to Albi, so inwardly at least, she probably didn't feel so enthusiastic. We were so grateful for her giving us such a great start.

We had a long, but enjoyable first day and made fantastic progress – setting off from St. Jean Pied de Port at 7:30 am and arriving in Roncesvalles at 2 pm. Roncesvalles is recognized as the first stop over point on the Camino Frances. It is a small hamlet, with a huge Hostel (formerly a monastery) and a single restaurant. Its elevated position in The Pyrenees coupled with our March 31st start date, made it a very chilly first stop on the Camino. As we were early and the hostel didn't open till 4 pm, and with the weather dry, but very chilly, we decided to do a little bit more walking and ended up in Burguete, one and a half hours later - A total distance of approximately 27-30 km walked.

The first day of walking was both exciting and long. The camaraderie between the 4 of us was instant and we covered the taxing incline of over 4,000 feet of Pyrenean ascent in good spirits. This was despite the fact that I had slept fitfully the night before as my companions known, and unknown, had snored though the night. My lack of sleep can only be partly blamed on the nocturnal rumblings of my fellow pilgrims. I had been suffering with some sort of cold (I thought it was a chest infection) as we had progressed towards departure day and so I was physically a little low as we set off from St Jean.

We had no choice but to follow the 'Valcarlos' route out of St Jean as our preferred path, the 'Route de Napoleon' on the high mountain passes wouldn't officially open till 1st of April, which was a day too late for us. We had contemplated defying that route closure advice, but instead made the wise decision to conform to unwritten but long observed and respected Camino regulation and stick to the routes that were marked as open. We found out later that day that 2 Brazilian Pilgrims who risked the Napoleon route the week before had to be rescued by helicopter as they got lost in deep snow drifts up on the mountain. Allegedly, their insurance didn't cover the cost as they had defied local advice: a very expensive mistake.

The last 3 kilometres up to Roncesvalles were hot and with the temperatures reaching 28 degrees Celsius we had a real sweat on as we reached the summit. The views were extensive and breathtaking and provided real compensation for the energy expended during those last few hours of uphill trudge. We passed our first official signpost to Santiago: we only had 787 km to go. Given all the challenges of our first day I was therefore more than satisfied when we managed to walk those first 30 km without too much trouble. It perhaps made me push on a little further than was wise. This proved to be a mistake; our first on the Camino itself if you ignore the hob free hostel moment in St Jean the night before!

Unbeknown to us, Burguete had no hostels or restaurants so we were faced with 3 choices: walking another 6 km to the next village, which we didn't fancy, sleeping on the street which definitely didn't appeal or staying in higher end accommodation at a higher cost. We chose the latter, a Bed and Breakfast in the village, where we also had no option but to pay the owner to feed us!

Instead of our bed and meal costing us a budgeted €60 for the 4 of us, it cost over €160! On the plus side, we did enjoy our last bath for a month, even if it was only 1 metre long. As all four of us are over 6 feet tall we needed to show individual resourcefulness to successfully wash our hair, squeezing our 6 foot plus bodies into a bath no longer than our arms! That was the day, we mastered the 'Burguete Bathing Technique' which required you to lie on your back, head underwater for rinsing, with legs climbing the tiled walls high above the taps. Unedifying perhaps, but we were learning quickly that adaptation to our circumstances was going to be a key part of completing (and enjoying) our Camino.

Another Camino lesson was repeatedly learned that day; plan carefully and always give yourself a range of sleepover and food options in the location you aim for. A lesson learned and quickly digested.

DISTANCE TRAVELLED: 30 km
DISTANCE TO SANTIAGO: 769 km

Chapter Two

Saturday 1ˢᵗ April 2017
Camino Day Two: Burguete to Arre

Camino lesson Number 2. Read the travel guide carefully, and always give yourself escape routes.

It became clear in those first 2 days that we were good walkers and that every day we would make good times and distances as long as we looked after ourselves. The 4 of us shared common characteristics. We are all tall, we walk at a similar speed and we all walk fast. This meant that we were already able to walk faster than any other pilgrims we met.

On one hand this was fantastic; we made our target destinations much quicker than the guidebook suggested but on the other hand, it created an attitude of let's keep moving and gain territory. This took its toll on me as I was still feeling the effects of that chest infection. It also meant that we focused all our efforts on reaching one particular hostel in Zabaldika, run by 'singing nuns'. A decision on successive days that bounced back on us.

We arrived at 4 pm and made our discovery the hostel was shut, just as the travel guide had warned......we had just forgotten to take notice of the fact! It wouldn't open for the Camino season for another 2 weeks.

Whilst initially a bit peeved at the hostel closure, we more than made up for it. We were boosted and rejuvenated by our 'find of the day.' Above the hostel at Zabaldika was a small church where pilgrims, upon production of their pilgrim passport were allowed up the bell tower and could even ring the bell! The spiral staircase and floor boards in the church tower were definitely dangerous, there was no way in Health and Safety conscious Britain, that we could have gone up a church tower in a similar condition back home.

We even managed to gain an extra sneaky stamp from the old lady running the church that day. In order to qualify for a 'Compostela' or certificate of completion in Santiago, the Pilgrim has to gain a daily ink stamp from a hostel or Camino related attraction along the route. You have to physically prove that you have walked it!

The opportunity to ring the bell was a special moment. The deep, booming ring bounced across the valley.

Harry in particular loved it and it raised all of our spirits as we faced an extra enforced march to our overnight albergue.

We had no choice but to carry on for another 4 km in the rain, to the next town which was Arre. This meant that on Day 2 we walked a total of 35 km.

As you can imagine we were all pretty tired but doing this little bit of extra distance gave us a great head start for the next few days, especially, as at the back of my mind was the knowledge that in those first 12 days we had to try and save a day and a half of the stages that were suggested by our travel guide. Both Harry and Dan had to be in Burgos by April 11th to enable them to connect with flights and buses back to Loughborough and Toulouse Universities. University exams wait for no man and both of the boys had to be back on campus before Jake and I even reached the half way point of our Camino. We needed to walk 325 km in 12 days in order for them to make their connections, hence the urgency to push on.

In those first 2 days of our Camino-related effort we had already claimed back over half a day on official guidebook timings. On Day 2 we walked for 9.5 hours.

The walking on Day 2 was undulating, often muddy, sublimely peaceful and pretty. We were repeatedly wished 'Buen Camino' which surprisingly never grated. We enjoyed regular treats during the day, which included

Kendal Mint Cake supplied by Nicky from my school, which I had deliberately saved for our first challenging moment and Haribo provided by Jenny, Jake and Harry's grandma. We were now 11 km ahead of the guidebook and had made an 8 km gain on the day.

I learned some more things that day. I learned that I have 2 great sons and a great nephew. They didn't bicker or moan and they kept going even when it got tough or we faced a setback such as the hostel closure at Zabaldika. I also learned that despite travelling light, we could have actually economised further on our clothing. We really didn't need all of it. Our cotton 'Brain Tumour Research and Support' (BTRS) charity T shirts, were too heavy to wear and so an unnecessary weight in our packs. That said, those T-shirts were great PR for our cause when we eventually rolled into Santiago.

I also realised that more planning of our route was necessary to ensure a good hostel choice and local 'buy as you go' food options were always available. I resolved to never again leave us without food and accommodation choices during this Camino. As we all reflected that night, sore feet and aching limbs apart, all was 'Bueno' so far and our spirits remained high.

The hostel in Arre was just like those depicted in the film 'The Way', which had been our initial lure of 'The Camino de Santiago.' The hostel, on arrival, seemed to be shut. It wasn't. It was situated at the back of an old church and was pretty basic with washing lines strung between old and rusting bunk beds. The flaky WIFI only worked back in the church entrance which was at the other end of the building, but it still gave us an opportunity to FaceTime Nicky at home and share some quality time with her, albeit over the internet.

Finding the Church entrance for the aforementioned WIFI was always a challenge for me personally as it was serviced from the hostel by a maze of corridors which I for one, never seemed able to navigate.

Whilst basic, the hostel was clean-'ish' and had a free to use washing machine and tumble dryer. Given we hadn't washed any clothing in our first 3 days and were wearing our last clean change of clothing, I took advantage of our early finish which was achieved by the shorter 25 km walking distance that day and completed a full kit wash for all 4 of us, a surprisingly relaxed business.

We ate communally with a crew of new 'Camino Buddies', including Marek from Poland and Maria from Czech Republic. They were great fun and had their own interesting reasons for walking the Camino. Marek had a personal motivation to get to Santiago quickly. An ex professional footballer aged just 25, he had been forced to have both knees fully replaced 2 years earlier. His doctor was adamant that Marek would never walk again, and the Camino was Marek's personal objective in disproving that doctor's medical opinion. His stated intent even on Day 2 was to send his doctor a postcard from Santiago in less than 3 weeks' time.

We thought we were making good progress, but our achievements paled into insignificance when we were to learn that Marek averaged 40 km each day and finally made Santiago in a total of 23 days, 5 days ahead of Jake and me. To walk it on plastic knees was jaw-droppingly impressive, especially as our knees were already killing us after just 2 days. It seemed at the time we were in Arre and over the next 2 days as we retained contact with him, that Marek might slow down as there seemed to be a possible interest of the romantic sort in Maria. This failed to materialise though, and we later heard on the Camino bush telegraph that Marek had blazed ahead, and that Maria had caught a bus for the infamous Meseta section between Burgos and Leon. We didn't see either of them again on our Camino but heard from and still receive periodic updates from Marek via Facebook.

DISTANCE TRAVELLED: 65 km
DISTANCE TO SANTIAGO: 734 km

Chapter Three

Sunday 2nd April 2017
Camino Day Three: Arre to Uterga

As far as distance goes, we enjoyed a slightly shorter day of it - around 25 km on Day 3. We were elated, still ahead of schedule by about 12 km which remained great going.

We walked from Arre to Uterga (via Pamplona.) It was another great day, and despite some sore limbs our high spirits remained, and the improving weather was a bonus.

The highlight of the day was definitely the sculptures on 'Alto del Perdon', The Hill of Forgiveness, which we had first seen in the film. To actually sit astride those bronze sculptures high above the Plains of Pamplona, felt very special.

The boys all walked well, we had retained a reasonable level of control on the blisters that were starting to afflict us all. My best pre-Camino investment had been 6 packs of 'compeed' blister plasters. I had read repeatedly prior to starting the Camino, that prevention of blisters, was the most important piece of planning that a Pilgrim could adopt. I had been insistent that if a blister started to appear, we would stop and treat it, to prevent worsening. It didn't help our cause though that Harry had arrived on Camino with at least 5 already well-established blisters, caused by Loughborough University's requirement that students wear full safety boots, in the design studios. These studios had been his daily home base from 9-5 pm for the 4 weeks preceding our starting the Camino and wearing those safety boots had definitely taken a toll on his feet. He never moaned though.

Our various afflictions were as follows: Harry had blisters, about 8, but all of these were under control on Day 3. Jake's knee was now hurting him and so he started to wear the knee support I had been given by my Mum who lives in France. I had taken the precaution of taking these out to Spain with me, as I had been diagnosed with early osteoarthritis in both knees in January 2016; though thankfully I never needed them. Dan was also struggling with blisters caused by his brand-new walking boots which he hadn't had time to break in. I was still struggling with the effects of a cold and the persistent dry cough was affecting my ability to sleep every night and probably everyone else's too.

That night we stayed in a very clean, privately owned albergue in Uterga run by a lady we nicknamed Donna. She was a 'look alike' in appearance and behaviour to Donna, our good neighbour and friend back in Halifax.

There were no kitchen facilities in this hostel and no local shops, so we resorted to the Pilgrim Menu at €10 each which was perfect.

At the end of Day 3 we had maintained our daily average of 30 km.

A final word on Jake. I was astonished at his resilience. Just over 13 months ago he had been struggling to recover from lifesaving brain surgery. He needed to use a wheelchair for 8 weeks after his surgery. Yet here he was walking over 30 km every day, striding out, often in front of us all; a living example of bravery, fortitude, strength of character and stamina on this arduous challenge.

DISTANCE TRAVELLED: 90 km
DISTANCE TO SANTIAGO: 709 km

Chapter Four

Monday 3rd April 2017
Camino Day Four: Uterga to Estella

It was a much sunnier day on Day 4 and Harry's complexion was now as red as a beautiful Spanish sunrise. More seriously, we were always sensible with the sun which could easily burn you, even in early April. Despite the cold early mornings where I had to wear hat and gloves, by 11 am we were always downsizing to shorts and T-shirts and always conscientiously applied lotion. That Spanish sun, even in early spring was hot. So, whilst we were tanning nicely, thankfully we never got sunburnt.

We were loving every minute of this trek, even the hard and hot slog in the early afternoons when we really only wanted to arrive at our next lodgings. We had already met some great people and had started to wonder if we could meet a nationality beginning with each letter of the alphabet. South Koreans seemed to be the most numerous of Pilgrims, after the Spanish of course.

This was a pretty and interesting section of the Camino with small towns and villages dotted along the trail every 4/5 km. This kept the walks stimulating and allowed us to grab a reward, usually of the edible kind, whenever we wanted to. It also helped us secure a 'Pilgrim Rhythm.' Typically, we would be up, showered and out by 7:30 am usually walking in the cold morning light of dawn.

Before leaving our overnight accommodation, we would enjoy a shared box of cereal: always demolished between the 4 of us as we resolved early on that if we could avoid it, we would not carry extra weight.

At around 0:900, just like hobbits, from the Tolkien novels, we would stop for a second breakfast having usually completed a 12 km stretch of our daily target. We would then check in with home, family or friends via WIFI in the cafe, recharge our phones and still be on our way, dressed down into shorts by 10:15 with at least 1 and a half hours of further walking before the heat of the Spanish spring, started to really hit us.

Day 4 was a little different to our previous days however, as there had been no supermarket in or around Donna's albergue, for us to buy the cornflakes we typically enjoyed for our 'first breakfast' every morning. We had the unwelcome experience of needing to walk 7 km to the next village before we could buy breakfast. Donna was way too relaxed for an early riser Camino Pilgrim, she didn't serve breakfast till 08:30 which was far too late for us. Despite this challenge, we managed to complete our first 'Survival Skills: Camino Style' film before breakfast as well. These films may be of limited interest to the reader, but they were great fun to make, and worthwhile to the four of us at least.

To summarise the film; I basically staggered around Obanus under Jake's direction, with Harry filming. I had to pretend that I was at death's door through a lack of water. I staggered into a courtyard in front of the old church and approached my last point of potential help;

an old well. As I pleaded "I'm in Obanus, I need water… It's a ghost town!", Jake and Dan, hidden and pre-positioned inside the dry well threw out 2 water bottles which I caught expertly in our one and only 'take'.

We posted the 50 second film on social media. It got a good reaction even if it really was very silly. It reinforced a personal perspective that Jake's illness and his subsequent attitude had increasingly influenced on me; try not to take life too seriously!

Our breakfast of 2 croissants each tasted particularly good after those filming heroics. Later during that day, our pace did drop a little, unsurprising in a sense as we had completed over 100 km in just 3 and a half days.

We re-established contact with Marek and Maria who had set out before us. Maria had inadvertently left her camera at a village a few miles back and so had to run back for it, whilst Marek looked after her rucksack.

Our last pull into Estella was tough. The signpost to the hostel said 3 km but we were sure it was more like 6 km and we began to develop a deep distrust of those Spanish hostel directional signs. We had hostels galore to choose from but chose the only 'donativo'. This is a hostel where you give a donation based on what you can afford and think the overnight stay was worth. It is also a common experience in most donativo hostels to eat communally.

The Estella donativo didn't provide a communal meal, instead I took one for the team and cooked for us; purchasing chicken, rice and vegetables from a local supermarket and then sharing what we cooked with a few other pilgrims.

We went to bed that night, satisfied if a little sore. Our satisfaction levels were particularly high because we had walked yet another 30+ kilometres. The hostel in Estella was the best yet. It was run by Betty, an Irish lady acting as 'hospitallero' with an Australian lady called Elaine. They were sweet, kind and helpful. Nothing was ever too much to ask.

They marvelled at Jake's story and kept asking him more questions. He loved the attention and was quite happy to chat and avoid the fact that his sweaty socks and underwear were waiting to be washed. That was becoming my sole privilege and my own daily perk! The albergue in Estella was our second donativo experience and we were starting to adopt a policy of deliberately hunting them out. They seemed to attract a different type of Pilgrim; the type who wanted to scratch deeper into the experiences that 'The Way' provides. These were people who wanted to chat, discuss things at a deeper level; not always seriously 'deep' conversations, but certainly discussions that showed a person's personality in more depth or revealed more about their culture, attitudes and customs. The donativo hostels really were proving to be the best, for us at least.

The hostel was clean, but only had one bathroom with shower and toilet and needed to be shared between 16 pilgrims! This presented obvious potential 'supply and demand' issues in the morning. We weren't too bothered about that though. We always seemed to be amongst the early risers and we always managed to remain clean.

That night we mixed with a number of more familiar pilgrims, Davinia, aged 22 was from Barcelona and Susannah from Indonesia who had lived in Spain for a year. Elaine a Geordie living near Lake Tahoe in the USA and Jaco her Dutch walking companion. Susannah and Elaine were kind enough to donate to our BTRS charity when they heard Jake's story. It reminded me of just how many people still have an ability to be moved by a story like Jake's, compassion and kindness were never far from us on the trail; Elaine and Susannah were just the latest to show it to us on the Camino.

Elaine's story was a real-life drama of its own. She had originally started her walk on the Camino del Norte, intending to hug the northern coastline of Spain until dropping down into Santiago. Just 2 days before we met up with her, whilst on this walk, she was seriously intimidated by the behaviour of a jogger who exposed himself to her, twice on the same day. Elaine felt threatened enough to defend herself with a knife and on the joggers third appearance had been hugely relieved at the timely arrival of the police. Her description of her assailant had led to his arrest and after a long day of giving statements and a successful identity parade, she had decided to break south and take the Camino Frances. This route had numerous pilgrims in comparison to the quiet northern route where at this time of year you could easily travel a day without seeing another walker. Her attitude was fantastic. She had survived a very scary and intimidating experience in a very isolated location, yet she chose to continue to walk. She adapted her plans to enable her to still travel as a single woman, but with a greater sense of personal safety and security.

By the time we had reached Estella we had completed a further 30 km and gained a whole day on the recommended guidebook route stages and their associated timings. We had finished the Guidebook's 5th stage in just 4 days. This was a great feeling as it had put us well on track for Dan and Harry to make their home connections on the 11th April.

By the end of Day 4 we were now hardy 'Camino Peregrinos' with over 100 km completed and it felt to us like Santiago was getting closer every day.

We went to bed that night, satisfied if a little sore.

DISTANCE TRAVELLED: 120 km
DISTANCE TO SANTIAGO: 679 km

Chapter Five

Tuesday 4th April 2017
Camino Day Five: Estella to Torres del Rio

Day 5 proved to be the hardest day yet, there were long stretches of road within a featureless and less exciting landscape and the sun started beating down on us at about 12 noon, making us very hot and bothered. Nonetheless, we made it to Torres after nine and a half hours of walking (7:30 am – 5 pm). We all felt the effects of our efforts on this stretch and resorted to lots of breaks, which resulted in slower progress.

Despite this it was a good day and we maintained our 30 km average! The next day anticipated a leisurely 21 km walk so we all looked forward to that as a bit of a 'rest day'.

We stopped at the iconic red wine fountain 6 km beyond Estella where we sampled the local vintage which is offered freely to pilgrims by the principle wine producer of the region. To me it really tasted vile and at 9 am was totally unpalatable. We bid Elaine a farewell with a mutual toast at the fountain.

The walk to Los Arcos mid-morning was a lovely one; lush green fields a beautiful sky and we met a tiny Peruvian lady named Anne Marie and Stefan, a bearded German with the most ferocious penknife I have ever seen. With that knife in his hand, I would have defied even the SAS to confront him!

By noon the temperature had become very hot and the walk onto Los Arcos involved another 12 km without a town or village to break the journey. The straight path of the Camino stretched on miles into the distance and for a short while we had significant 'bike envy', as pilgrims in the saddle sped past us.

We briefly hooked up with an American we nicknamed 'Seattle Henry' who proved to be a decent walking companion, despite some initial reservations on my part. This again reminded me, not for the first time on this Camino, that I should always reserve my judgement of a fellow human being and never 'judge a book by its cover.' We had realized quite quickly that chatting to fellow pilgrims could often prove to be a useful distraction, especially when things started to get tough.

The last 2 km from Los Arcos into Torres del Rio was the toughest yet on our Camino. For me my chest problem was now making a hard walk feel harder still. The greater the exertion, the greater my dry cough and I found this stage of the Camino a really tough one.

It was with real relief that we arrived at our hostel for the night. We had walked another 30 km with some difficulty and had completed a 5th of the whole Camino.

DISTANCE TRAVELLED: 155 km
DISTANCE TO SANTIAGO: 644 km

Chapter Six

Wednesday 5th April 2017
Camino Day Six: Torres del Rio to Logroño

Torres del Rio proved to be an average stopover, certainly nothing special. The hostel whilst clean was run as a business. There was consequently less of the spirit of generosity that was so prevalent in the donativo hostels that we had stayed in. To us they always seemed to be friendlier and more welcoming.

After leaving the hostel, we had to walk for our breakfast again; this time over 2 hours to Viano, about 14 km. When we arrived, we ensured we feasted like kings with a double breakfast of croissants, orange juice and strong local coffee. We had made good time, which was all the more welcome as Jake had clearly suffered yesterday. Today his knee was a little better and he walked at a good pace, again showing the grit and determination that had been so apparent within the context of the 2 years of his illness.

I too had slept well, exhaustion does that to you. The combination of being physically shattered from the walking and the last 10 days of really poor sleep, meant that I slept through the night, making me feel better than previous days. I did reflect that maybe we were finally getting our 'Camino legs.' Added to this was the fact that the walk on Day 6 was significantly shorter which was perhaps a psychological boost to us all. We had finished walking before 1 pm which provided us all with valuable downtime.

Whilst the scenery of Rioja wasn't the prettiest; the region of Navarra was much nicer. It was easier walking and the only difficulty we had when we arrived in Logroño, which is a sizeable town, was finding somewhere to buy bread and cheese for a simple self-sufficient lunch. Dan ended spending a whole euro on a solitary onion which was neither a good indication of his thriftiness, or a positive reflection of his Spanish interpretation or a celebration of his entrepreneurial skills.

We stayed in the donativo hostel attached to the church right in the town centre. After the much gentler walk of only 20.5 km we were all feeling much better!

I was able to employ my latest 'treat initiative' for the boys, who certainly deserved a bit of pampering. We headed off for a sneaky relax in the 'Polideportivo', a Spanish Sports Centre complete with swimming pools and spas.

The boys loved their treat: 2 hours of sauna and jacuzzi. Jenny, Harry and Jake's grandma had had the bright idea and we lavished our praises in her direction for that great wisdom. She had felt it would rejuvenate us and she was correct. The combination of ice baths, plunge pools combined to make it an enjoyable and memorable few hours afternoon break.

We did however, appear to irritate a local by having our Go Pro camera in the pool for some covert, undercover filming of our next silly short film. We flatly refused to allow 'Señor Grumpy' to spoil our next 'Spielberg-esque' sequel, even if it was possibly even more silly than the last. We based the film within the swirling waters of the jacuzzi and named it 'Rejuvenation.'

We had now crossed out of Navarra and we were in the famous wine region of La Rioja. This felt like a significant milestone along the journey, and we proffered our thanks to Navarra, and then bid it 'Adiós'.

After witnessing the generosity of Susanna and Elaine who in Estella, we heard of even more generosity back home, from the Rotary Club of Halifax. The group had donated £200 to BTRS with further generous individual donations from their members based in Halifax. This meant that we had now broken the £10,000 barrier with our fundraising on just Day 6 of the walk. Our initial target total had been £5,000 so we felt elated that we had already smashed that total and were well on our way to £11,000. We felt an overwhelming sense of gratitude to our sponsors. Whilst still recognising the reality that this challenge was tough It was also proving to be an epic experience.

That night we looked forward to a communal meal with the other pilgrims. We were all feeling good.

We now had a strategy to deliberately stay in donativo hostels and our stay at the donativo hostel in Logroño was superb. Roberto and his wife Elsie had run the hostel for the previous 16 years, as volunteer hospitalleros.

I frequently work with volunteers in my job as a Headteacher. We have some magnificently loyal volunteers who are hugely generous with their time and support. Roberts and Elsie were of the same ilk. They were unbelievably hospitable, generous and kind; giving 4-6 months to volunteering each year for the past 16 years. Uprooting and living in an old, dusty hostel many miles from home, cooking and providing for a group of different pilgrims every night, carries a remarkable level of commitment. They clearly loved their vocation, but their sheer humility and compassion for people who would only cross their paths for a few brief hours and who on most occasions they would never see again, was mind blowing. They gently professed their Christian faith without cringe factor or exaggerated zeal. More importantly they demonstrated their faith in action, the reference in the bible "You will know them by their fruits" Matthew chapter 7 vs 16 (NIV) sprang to mind. I reflected that night on their superb generosity of spirit. Volunteering on the Camino was the life they had chosen as a couple ever since they retired. They provided us with the most magical experience of the whole Camino.

Before the evening meal we sang the Camino Anthem of which we were unaware. The words had no meaning to us (though we could guess the intent) but we sang with gusto and enthusiasm all the same. It obviously spoke of patience, kindness and 'the Camino will provide'.

There were 14 of us for a communal meal of 'Patatas a la Riojana', a very tasty potato and chorizo dish preceded by salad with olives and sunflower seeds and we English boys relished second and third helpings, the long-distance walking was making us very hungry and for the remainder of the Camino we were never fed as well as on that night.

I think our stay in Arre was our first truly spiritual moment and it was felt by everyone who stayed there together that night. We had people of faith and no faith in that company; in later conversations a professed atheist in the group recognised that this evening had a truly special third dimension to it.

The contemplation element of the evening took place in the old church attached to the hostel by a series of candle lit, underground tunnels. Roberto led us through them into the dark unlit church, where we sat in a circle in mystical candlelight on ornately carved wooden pews that were clearly hundreds of years old.

Roberto confessed that on a previous evening he had managed to lose 3 Italian pilgrims in the tunnels leading into the church; an admission which provoked great laughter, born from the realism that this was profoundly possible and very likely true. In a short 10 minute study and contemplation, we shared the same reading about the Camino in 4 languages: Spanish, English, German and French. Dan was delegated to do the French reading.

The conversations after the service in the church, as we washed up and prepared the table for the communal breakfast on the next morning were littered with laughter. Roberto had taken our Camino friendships to a totally new level.

That night we were challenged by Roberto to forget the desire to complete 'The Way' and instead focus on 'Growing and Going' as we progressed along it. He said 'The Way' itself was unimportant, what was important was how we developed individually as we walked along it. It really was a super special moment, made all the better by the wonderful companionship we were starting to share with our fellow and now increasingly familiar pilgrims. A bond had clearly begun to form. We were now starting to travel together intentionally as a modern day 'Band of Brothers'. There were now 9 of us and we had already stayed together for over 24 hours.

There was an obvious comparison for me as we started to travel together, that of my favourite book, 'The Lord of the Rings', by JRR Tolkien. We were now becoming a nine strong 'Community of the Camino', just like Frodo and his travelling companions who had formed the nine strong 'Fellowship of the Ring'. Maintaining a near average of 30 km per day, meant that we were now over a quarter of the way to Santiago.

Day 6 was significant for a number of reasons and not just for the impact made by Roberto and Elsie. They were a key and central influence though. It was a day that was definitely enhanced by the fun we were enjoying with our new Camino companions and the communal meals we enjoyed together.

DISTANCE TRAVELLED: 175.5 km
DISTANCE TO SANTIAGO: 623.5 km

Chapter Seven

Thursday 6th April 2017
Camino Day Seven: Logroño to Nájera

On Day 7 we managed another great shift and walked 31 km, meaning we had managed 196 km in 7 days. We really motored, completing a seven and a quarter hour stage 40 minutes earlier than the guidebook predicted. This early finish allowed us, or should I say me, to wash all of our clothes; 3 days of smelly socks were scrubbed by me alone (once again), my socks, unlike those of the boys were beautiful of course!

The second part of the day's walking was quite tough as for several kilometres we followed a path next to a motorway, only separated from the fast-moving cars by a chain link fence. On arrival Nájera appeared to be a total dump. Thankfully the old part of town was lovely.

We all felt that on Day 7 we had definitely found our Camino legs. Yes, we did have some blisters, aching joints and sore feet, but we were also confident walkers who knew that barring a major mishap, we could handle most circumstances that the Camino could throw at us. The experience was proving to be so much fun travelling as a foursome, when you enhanced it with the shared banter from our travelling companions and the wonderful hospitality, we had received the previous night, it became a whole new level of experience.

The donativo breakfast that morning had been superb, and I enjoyed the luxury of 4 coffees! No instant rubbish in this hostel. This was strong coffee that provided the caffeine inspired buzz that I needed for the long walk that day. It certainly helped as we walked well, covering over

18 km in just 3 hours, meaning we made Nájera by 2.30 pm allowing us a welcome ice-cold cola drink in a café, next door to our next donativo hostel, which was a much bigger affair than in Logroño. Once again it was brilliantly run by the most helpful of volunteer hospitalleros, this time a gentleman from Canada.

Our strategy of walking well, fast and with intent was paying huge dividends. The boys had needed licking into shape. It had taken some time and persistent nagging from me but as week 2 of our Camino started, but they were now so much more efficient in how they packed their gear up. They discovered the benefit of easy to locate plasters and scissors for blisters. Careful top of the rucksack access meant quick treatment was often reinforced by a stash of edible treats similarly well positioned. They now packed their rucksacks strategically and they knew where things were and located them with ease. They also understood that by getting to a hostel early they could choose the best beds, get first access to the washing facilities and enjoy extended chill time. They could perhaps play cards, relax, listen to music, chat to other walkers or write up their journals. This, coupled with superb weather, meant that we were always a happy crew of travellers. There was simply no bickering. We enjoyed each other's company and had heaps of fun.

Harry cooked that night, making a delicious Mexican meal which we again shared with some of our companions. The walk on day 7 was only 20 km but we knew if we added a further voluntary 6 km, we could stay in a highly recommended donativo in Grañon. Our donativo sourcing strategy was now secured. They provided such a cultural high as opposed to the more business orientated private hostels where making a profit was the obvious, if never actually stated, policy.

By cracking on at this stage and walking some extra distance, there was always the attractive possibility of a second spa treat in Burgos before the boys left. They had loved the experience so much in Logroño, that it seemed sensible to try to repeat it.

What had I learnt in the first week of the Camino?

I realised that loved my boys unconditionally and I loved their sheer tenacity.

I began to understand that I also needed to grow and develop in so many areas; I have many 'rough edges' that need knocking off.

I realised that I missed Nicky and my 22 year old daughter Rosie very much and that their absence was the only thing missing from this magical experience. Finally,

I knew that I was loving being a Pilgrim and having a long-distance path ahead of me, with an ending that was still 3 weeks away. My woes, travails and work-related challenges were being buried in the dust of the Camino and my mind was increasingly detoxing every day.

DISTANCE TRAVELLED: 206.5 km
DISTANCE TO SANTIAGO: 593.5 km

Chapter Eight

Friday 7th April 2017
Camino Day Eight: Nájera to Grañon

Easter Sunday is in 9 days and so we are considering our options for where we would like to spend it. As a historically Catholic country with all the cultural traditions of this faith still deeply embedded in Spain, we thought it would be interesting to be based somewhere prominent so that we could potentially spectate at a town fiesta, where communal Easter processions were definitely more likely to take place. Coupled with that was our desire to stay at a highly recommended donativo hostel in Grañon, where pilgrims could enjoy another communal meal and actually sleep in the church bell tower. The guidebook distance for our day was 20.5 km but we had 6 more kilometres to walk if we did decide to head for that hostel.

Having done a full wash in Nájera, we travelled clean and had no washing to sort until we would have to say goodbye to Harry and Dan in Burgos. It amused me to witness how the boys were readily available to give me their dirty washing but suddenly went missing when the actual handwashing began. It reminded me of my brother Simon, their uncle, who in our childhood days, always disappeared to the toilet after a meal, just as the washing up was about to start. I did wonder ruefully, whether he had introduced this avoidance strategy to my boys on the night before we left for Biarritz. We had stayed with Simon and his wife Liz as they live less than 40 minutes from Stansted airport, making a stress-free morning departure for our Camino a very attractive prospect.

I didn't mind them missing on the hand washing too much. I quite like the concept of completing acts of service and it was actually quite nice to get some personal downtime. At worst I would have 8 pairs of walking socks, 8 sets of underwear and 8 T-shirts to wash by hand. There were also the towels, which often got smelly very quickly.

In fact, in my school, I have introduced a weekly assembly focus where we celebrate 'Random Acts of Kindness' from students or staff. It was very much within that spirit, that I figured I would be a bit of a hypocrite if I didn't practice what I preached. So, the washing was done, and I made no complaints about their convenient absences. Besides it enabled me to ensure that my fellow travellers were never smelly pilgrims.

On Day 8 we made good ground covering 27 km in 5 and a half hours walking time. We chose to walk the extra 6 km to stay in the church and it was definitely worth it. It was a hot walk in the afternoon and I finally decided to see a local doctor to get my 2-week-old cough checked out. This meant we were an hour delayed but on the positive side I now had a prescription which hopefully would settle down that oh so irritating cough. The flip side was that the prescribed powder sachets that I was instructed to take three times daily, were the most-evil tasting medication I have been offered. Nothing could mask the flavour especially the hint of lemon which accompanied the bitter taste of bile. I tolerated the medication for 2 days but finally ditched the remaining sachets in the donations box of a hostel further down the trail. My irritating and persistent dry cough was infinitely more preferable to that disgusting white powder.

My cough was identified as just a cough and not a chest infection by the doctor, meaning I received some 'attention seeker' and 'time waster' jibes from the boys. I was still glad to check it out. After 2 weeks of coughing whenever I lay down, I really wanted to see its demise. At the hostel, we again played the 'strategy game'. Even as we took our rucksacks off in our sleeping quarters, which was actually a mezzanine floor in the Church tower, where we slept on thick mats, I was scooping up the clothing for our hand washing.

Our now established and routine 'early arrival strategy' meant that we nearly always got first option on the hostel washing facilities or washing machine (if that luxury actually existed.) Other pilgrims who arrived later, often found themselves queuing for over an hour and with that the ensuing drying time reduction as the afternoon heat dissipated. Whilst they queued and laboured in the late afternoon sun, we were once again, nearly always done and dusted. This time I had the luxury of a machine to use and for a €3 wash cycle and €2 dryer time it really was a simple choice to make.

As ever, the boys were oblivious to this washing strategy. It mattered not, I knew that the strategy worked every time and gave us a clear organisational and time advantage over our fellow pilgrims, even if my companions seemingly knew nothing about it.

The walk to Grañon was a good one. Given I had long harboured some secret fears that by this stage the novelty of walking the seemingly never-ending Camino might have worn off and the boys might have become bored by it, it was so uplifting to see them walk with spirit and gusto. The banter was great; we rarely walked in silence and the implementation of the concept of rucksack rotation every hour was also a good one. It just gave us all a regular change that broke up any potential monotony.

Even with an irritating cough and with blisters on the feet of all 4 of us, we were still averaging well over 5 km an hour. In this way, coupled with an early start, we would often have blazed along the trail by late morning, almost always making us one of the first groups to check in to the next hostel usually no later than 3 pm. It gave us good amounts of resting and recovery downtime, which again helped to keep our individual and collective spirits high.

We all wore our boots despite each of us suffering with some controlled blisters. Harry chose to change into lightweight trainers after the first 15 km, tying his boots across the top of his rucksack, hanging loosely down each side. As a result, the rotating rucksacks policy wasn't quite as popular today as the carrier of his gear would often find that the rhythm of their own walking meant that they would get a regular boot to the ears as they swung like pendulums from the sides of his back pack. Once again we could tolerate this; each Pilgrim in our foursome would get at least 3 hours without the swinging boots before their hour of 'thick ears' arrived.

I have already alluded to the fact that our foot care policy had been embedded from the moment we had left St Jean Pied de Port and once again it was fully justified. Yes, we were troubled by blisters, but the application of a new blister plaster on a daily basis, coupled with our ability to rotate to wearing trainers if we wanted to, meant that they never threatened our ability to walk, or made walking a grim and painful business.

We stopped in Santa Domingo for one of our best lunch spots so far. It was a lovely day and the shaded square in the village centre provided us with some relief from the midday sun. Freshly purchased baguettes, grated cheddar cheese, chorizo, onion and tomato have never tasted so good. They were followed by ice creams and fresh strawberries; it really was a memorable lunch, made all the more special by its setting, the company and the complete simplicity of our Camino lives. When you walk up to 30 km every day, hunger and the thought of food is never far away and on that particular day we were ravenous.

Despite the hour delay for my appointment with the Spanish doctor, we arrived in Grañon at 3.15 pm, hot, bothered and out of fresh water but still very happy.

About a dozen pilgrims slept on camping mats in the bell tower that night. We were now hooked up with some regular Camino friends: Thomas and Stefan (with the massive knife) from Germany, Davinia and Manola (who speaks no English) from Spain and George, a Canadian ranger who works in the northernmost region of British Columbia, setting up camping spots for affluent tourists who wish to experience the isolating wilderness of North America. His ranger skills were to prove useful on more than one occasion.

So, it was that 9 of the bed spaces were taken up by our friendly group, with the other 3 occupied by Dave, a Canadian heart surgeon, who we would get to know much better a week or so later as we approached Cruz de Ferro, and by 2 elderly South Koreans, travelling separately. The man was lovely, spending time teaching Daniel Korean, even though he spoke no English. Dan has a real lust for learning languages and was in his element as he conversed with increasing fluency with our Spanish and German speaking buddies. The Korean lady proved to be the grumpiest pilgrim that we were to ever meet on the trail. She moaned, glared and tutted at our group incessantly throughout the evening. She became our official 'public enemy number one' and the we were all relieved when she retired to bed at around 8.15 pm. Perhaps she had just had a bad day? Whatever! Our ultimate moment of triumph would arrive about 4 hours later.

The mezzanine where we slept overlooked a communal area with wood burning stove, which was lit that night; it is still chilly in Spain in April once the sun has set. The hostel in Grañon was also managed by volunteer hospitalleros who stayed for up to 2 weeks and fed the visiting pilgrim's dinner and breakfast. Our meals, as ever in these types of hostels were funded by the generosity of the pilgrims who donated the night before. There was the opportunity to visit the church in the early evening to participate in a short service of contemplation and also an optional 7 pm mass.

During the time of contemplation, we each shared our motivations for walking the Camino and once again it was very special. It was candlelit and each Pilgrim, about 16 of us, was encouraged to express their gratitude in a few short sentences in their own language. The boys gave simple but very touching and thought-provoking reasons why they were grateful for the Camino experience. I remember Jake's was very simple but deeply profound. His gratitude was summed up in 3 words; "I am alive".

The shared meal was good, though not quite at the level of that provided by Roberto and Elsie back in Nájera.

After dinner and the washing up, Thomas played the tuneless and decrepit old piano. He is a highly intelligent guy with all sorts of skills and talents. His piano playing was superb, despite it being terribly out of tune and the setting in that Church tower, enhanced by the warming effects of the fire and the music made it magical.

The pay back moment for the grumpy Pilgrim duly arrived in the early hours of the morning. She was sleeping in the far corner of the mezzanine and got up just after midnight to visit the toilet. It was very dark on that elevated balcony with only the glowing embers of the fire in the wood burner allowing a faint glimmer of light. She successfully tiptoed down the aisle separating the sleeping pilgrims, 6 either side, and promptly tripped over my sleeping mat, landing spread eagled on top of me. The mezzanine literally shook with laughter as she disappeared sheepishly downstairs. Jake and Harry both conceded on the next morning that they had both gone to sleep with tears of laughter streaming down their cheeks. As for me, I was unhurt by the unexpected body slam. Thankfully this lady was pretty small, and our sleeping mats were at least 2 inches thick, meaning that most of the slam effect of her body falling on me was absorbed by the mat. I do remember going to sleep with my own amusing self-reflections. As I lay there in the twilight zone between consciousness and slumber, I was reminded that 'vengeance really is a dish best served cold!'

Jake and I were both very mindful that we had just 3 days left with Harry and Dan. This was very difficult for both of us to communicate about, as we knew, without needing to say it, that we were going to miss them like crazy. But as that departure day was next Tuesday and so still 3 full days away, we tried to park that unpleasant thought and focus on the special times we were sharing.

Day 8 had been a real 'Buen Camino' sort of day!

DISTANCE TRAVELLED: 233 km
DISTANCE TO SANTIAGO: 567 km

Chapter Nine

Saturday 8th April 2017
Camino Day Nine: Grañon to Tosantos

Day 9 was a relatively easy day's walking which at just 21 km in distance meant we were only 48 km from Burgos, our first significant checkpoint, with 2 full days of travel still available. We actually arrived at the hostel in Tosantos by 1:20 pm having taken lunch washed down with ice creams in Belorado.

We had now left the famous winemaking region of La Rioja and entered Castilla y León. This walk started with me breaking our own 'Burgos Agreement' as I shaved off my beard. At the start of our Camino we had all agreed to walk from St Jean to Burgos without shaving. Apparently, the boys believed my reason for breaking this pact was because their taunts of calling me Gandalf the Grey or Saruman the White every day wasn't too flattering. I maintained it was just too scratchy and made me look dishevelled. It was ironic that I got so much beard abuse from the boys. Daniel's attempts at beard growing were pitiful, I think I had detected the protrusion of just the single hair under his chin during the preceding 9 days. Jake's and Harry's attempts were more fluff than bristle. As ever though, a 'prophet is never welcome in his own land' and as the obvious King of this Camino I was an altogether easy mutual target for the Troublesome Trio. I of course, took it all in the spirit in which it was meant and fought fire with fire. The banter levels were elevated once again and with the input levels from our travelling companions lifting those levels even further, the day's walk progressed very enjoyably.

The nights chosen hostel was a donativo, giving us an opportunity for another communal meal and short service of reflection as well as a chance to watch the sunset from the local mountain top. Whilst spirits soared across our extended group, there was a tinge of real sadness for me as I heard that one of our key staff at school has suffered a close family bereavement.

Tony is a loyal and hardworking member of our staff team and a real pleasure to work with. He is never complicated, never one of the few who seem to revel in causing upset and distraction from the focus of the job. The loss of his wife, across the Easter weekend, was a poignant reminder that despite the bubble-like experience of our Camino world, where daily life is paired down to the most limited of choice-making and where the hardest decision you may make, is where to sleep that night, this bereavement was a stark reminder that there was still a real world out there where the most bitter of human experiences are felt by people I know and care about, on a daily basis. We may have been a long way from Halifax, but I truly hoped he knew that he and his family were in our thoughts and prayers.

The donativo hostel at Tosantos had once again been recommended to us, this time by the hospitalleros at Grañon. As our international friends were also travelling to that hostel it meant there was another potential night of great camaraderie. George, the pterodactyl-like Canadian was proving an interesting and likeable character. There was also a spiritual bond between the two of us as it became apparent that he too had a strong Christian faith. What I liked most though, was that he was such a character, funny, genuine and just a bit whacky.

So many people with a stark resistance towards people of faith seem to persist with promoting the stereotype that the modern-day Christian is frumpy, dour, boring and dull. George, admittedly, was sometimes randomly dressed but he was never dull, actually he possessed a comic genius without always intending to be funny. I know Harry in particular, developed a deep respect and appreciation for him which revealed itself in the way it always does with Harry; a relentless barrage of banter which George both accepted and fired back in equal measure.

It became apparent that Davinia and George were also going to break off at Burgos and the reality that we would miss them too meant that we were all the more determined to enjoy these last few days together. Davinia had taken time from work to walk this first section of the Camino and intended to return in subsequent years to walk the other sections.

My morning medication proved as disgusting as ever and even a repeated dose of the strongest caffeine on the Camino so far, could not camouflage the aftertaste. I took the medication and considered if it was time to ditch the remainder of the sachets. I reflected that the most bitter irony yet, could be the potential for this powder to give the worst type of side-effect; constipation. Whilst it was unlikely or at least the doctor hadn't informed me of the possibility, I was minded with typical British pessimism, that It would be just my luck!

Everyone continued to walk well, even though Daniel was suffering in silence with a swollen ankle. I think Daniel had perhaps suffered more than any of us of with his feet, but we never once heard him complain. He too had some quite nasty blisters and unlike the Moorman boys, didn't have a trainer alternative to wear instead of his boots. His boots had been brand new, purchased a few days before we set out and so his 'breaking in' of them had actually been in situ on the Camino. What we were doing was not normal British (or French) walking, we were walking long distances, day after day in hot weather and our feet were swelling up in a natural reaction to that heat. Despite his pain, Dan never moaned. I do suspect there were times when he wanted to stop and maybe even eject from the Camino, but to his credit he displayed a stoical determination never to quit. He reminded me of Captain Oates who accompanied Scott of the Antarctic on that fateful expedition. Happily, the analogy ends there. Oates died out on the bitterly cold icefields of the artic glaciers, Dan did what he set out to do and safely made his connections back to university in Toulouse when we reached Burgos.

The day's walking was pretty enough and more broken up by small towns and villages than previously. Every 3 km would see us enter some sort of hamlet, which helped a lot as these towns were interesting and gave us a psychological lift. Sometimes a path that disappears in a straight line into the horizon can be more daunting mentally, than an undulating terrain with plenty of ups and downs. The towns allowed for regular water stops and bottle fills in the fountains that pepper the Camino. All the water is drinkable.

By mid-morning Jake, Harry and I would do our usual thing and change down to shorts. Dan usually walked in long trousers all day. No doubt, life in Toulouse has made him more acclimatised to the hot continental weather whereas we northern-based English Boys sweated profusely. Our donativo breakfast sustained us till we got to Belorado which, as a town, was nothing special. There have been just a few towns that I will be happy to never revisit on the Camino but mostly the scenery and culture has been uplifting and sometimes jaw-droppingly beautiful.

We ate lunch in Belorado where Harry got a wagging finger tell off from a passing motorcyclist as he shinned up a plane tree.

We played 'Name that Tune' and sang for the last few kilometres to Tosantos, covering that 4.7 km in under 50 minutes. The hostel was another with sleeping mats with all nine of us in one communal room. In fact, our group of 9 travellers took over the whole of that hostel. It was immaculately clean and run all year round by Santiago

(James in English). James informed us that there was an expectation for pilgrims to help cook the communal meal and to be in the kitchen by 6 pm. As I wrote my journal that afternoon, I was acutely aware of the peace, tranquillity, silence and beauty of our surroundings. Bird song filled the air. I could also hear the boys giggling with their mates in the hostel. Wi-Fi informed me that Bristol City FC were 3-0 up against Wolverhampton Wanderers and reminded me again of the 'real' world back home. I didn't dare return to the Wi-Fi till the next day in case they had done the usual and capitulated and lost in typical Bristol City style.

We made another short and equally silly film as our third Camino production. Named 'Roadkill', we substituted Kendal mint cake for a dead bird that lay in the road side and I pretended to eat the bird's wing through sleight of hand. Jake's 'The Hobbit' imitation of a troll saying, 'What is it?' in a wheedling and snarling voice, was the highlight, along with his own answer, again in imitation of Grishnak, an orc in The Lord of The Rings. 'We can try!' is legendary in our household. It was again a film highlight here.

The hostel was great, the food tasty and the company great fun as the nine of us enjoyed another magical evening. George went to watch the sunset, the rest of us chose to stay in as we were too tired to venture out again after all our uphill trudges. Apparently, it was a spectacular sunset.

Postscript: Of great importance to the three Bristol City fans in our walking group was the news that they had held on to win 3-1 and so move 4 points clear of the relegation zone in English football's second division: The Championship. It seemed that in our absence BCFC were doing much better!

A near certainty for relegation in January, their chances of survival were looking increasingly good.

DISTANCE TRAVELLED: 263.5 km
DISTANCE TO SANTIAGO: 541.5 km

Chapter Ten

Sunday 9th April 2017
Camino Day Ten: Tosantos to Atapuerca

It might seem slightly arrogant to claim that a 28 km walk was easy! In the context of our Day 10 this was true, and we had cleared the day's walking by 2 pm. We seemed to have fully adjusted to The Camino! At one point we were walking at well over 6 km an hour.

We walked the first hour as a group though George, Davinia and Stefan then fell off the pace, only catching back up with us at the albergue in Atapuerca. We enjoyed a second breakfast after 6 km of walking. Whilst not great (the croissants were a bit tough) it did help us to bridge the 9 km gap to St Juan de Ortega.

The path over the hill was long, but our pace hit 7 km an hour when we realised at 11:30 am that today was a Sunday and we had just one hour to make some sort of village or town so we could get food. On a Sunday in Spain, all shops shut at 12:30 pm. We cracked the whip and kept our pace high only to stroll into St Juan and find there were no shops! No matter, 'the Camino always provides' and we found a small bar serving Bocadilllos, long panini like toasted sandwiches, full of chorizo and cheese. It was a simple, affordable and very tasty variation on a foot-long Subway meal!

It was the hottest day so far on our Camino, so we decided to walk with only a short rest as it was likely to get even hotter later. We made our hostel by mid-afternoon. I was now already into 'walking for 2' mode. Harry and Dan could go home with dirty washing, but Jake and I needed to keep a 'wash and go' policy. His philosophy seemed to be far more straightforward, 'wear and go' (and let dad do the washing!)

We were now just 19 km from Burgos.

Dan had the possibility of a train to Toulouse at 6 pm on Monday so we were well placed to make that option however sad the thought of it made us feel. Spirits were still high, but the knowledge that Dan and Harry were leaving gave us an unspoken and foreboding presence. It was also clear that Jake and I would then need to 'up our game' as we needed to manage at least 30 km for 17 days to make Santiago to meet the girls. We were so grateful our two pace setters who had done their job so well.

As I wrote up my diary that night, I realised that we had now walked over a third of our Camino. An average of 27 km a day would get us to Santiago one day before our flight back to the UK. Of course, we wanted to see a bit of Santiago and enjoy a bit of down time, after what would have been a gruelling challenge, so we knew that around 30 km a day would squeeze us in some rest days in Santiago. I was often pretty busy as I walked, doing the mathematics mentally and working out what our best accommodation option would be. I was also trying to calculate how we would play the day of Harry's departure from Santiago. He was aiming for a 2 pm departure on 11th April, which meant that Jake and I would lose a significant amount of time if we were to wait around Burgos to see him off. However, the thought of an easy day in Burgos was also very appealing. I even toyed with the idea of Jake and I doing an overnight walk after waving Harry goodbye. This sounded cool and I knew Jake would be up for it, but it would also knock our body clocks all over the place and the thought of losing a night's sleep was not quite so attractive! For the first time in over 10 days I would actually have to start to make some decisions. I had decided that I really was enjoying a decision free life, so in a fit of decisive indecision I decided that I would make that decision tomorrow!

This time we stayed in a decent private hostel and all of us caught up again on what was going to be our last night together. We used the hostel kitchen for Dan to cook pasta carbonara.

I slept well for the first time in over 2 weeks. The hostel was good and the hospitallero as obliging as any. We were also staying with established Camino friends and that made the evenings all the more relaxing.

George, the Canadian Ranger, came into his own that night. He really was a brilliant guy, though quite unconventional. I theorized that he was probably like this because he spent 6 months minimum each year on his own in the vast emptiness of the northern Canadian territories. The location sounded stunning but living in the wilderness for 6 months a year didn't sound like my cup of tea. Our hospitallero took a team photograph and as I studied it later it made me once again marvel at what the Camino provided. I knew that if I ever ended up in Germany, Barcelona or Canada, my Camino friends would be delighted to host me, and I would likewise host them should they ever come to the UK.

DISTANCE TRAVELLED: 296 km
DISTANCE TO SANTIAGO: 525 km

Chapter Eleven

Monday 10th April 2017
Camino Day Eleven: Atapuerca to Burgos

On Day 11 we knew we were going to say goodbye to my nephew Dan. We waved him off on his bus, on a journey back to Toulouse that would involve countless buses and trains totalling over 28 hours of travel time. Dan was a great Camino Pilgrim, he had excellent linguistic skills, was fun and never once complained. The team of 4 never fell out (although Harry and Jake had their moments with each other). We knew we were going to miss him. It was a real privilege to spend Camino time with our nephew/cousin. I reflected later that night as I started to drift off to sleep that my sister Lizzie and her husband Dave had every right to be proud parents, he really was a top lad!

It is very likely that saying goodbye to Dan was the real reason behind what felt like a tough day. What should have been an easy 20 km seemed to be very challenging and we all felt it. The walk into Burgos really was very dull. We reached the airport relatively easily, but the 10 km walk from there seemed to go on and on and on. A lie in didn't seem to have helped any of us. We had set off at 8 am a full hour and quarter later than normal, as our target distance was so small. We had a seemingly never-ending trudge through Burgos with no water fountains or kilometre signs to the city centre to encourage us.

Despite the challenge, we made it to the donativo hostel in Burgos. We were delighted to be there, but we were also gutted to lose Dan.

The donativo hostel really was 5* in every aspect. It was a beautiful modern design; light, airy and very uplifting. The hospitalleros were a middle-aged couple from West Virginia, USA. They cooked us a lovely meal of salad and lentil stew, with plenty of bread, and that rarity on the Camino - a lovely pudding.

The now familiar format for the evening followed with a spiritual exchange which we all found very uplifting. The 10 pilgrims staying in the hostel that night, were asked to share their reasons for doing the Camino. Given we were now mostly a group of strangers, we were all surprisingly honest and open. The shared personal stories meant that this became a very emotional experience for us all. After hearing Jake's story, Carl the American hospitallero, was quite emotional and I too found that I spoke with my emotions barely in check and with a very shaky voice. It was only 10 minute long reflection discussion, but it was a very powerful 10 minutes all the same.

DISTANCE TRAVELLED: 316 km
DISTANCE TO SANTIAGO: 483 km

Chapter Twelve

Tuesday 11th April 2017
Camino Day Twelve: Burgos to Hornillos del Camino

Day 12 was full of goodbyes; in the last 24 hours a group of 9 International Pilgrims had become just 2 English boys. It was a tough day all round; the principal reason being the decimation of our Band of Brothers.

I also knew that later on this day, we would be saying goodbye to Harry. I felt really quite tearful about that prospect. In our 11 days as a foursome we had walked a daily average of almost 29 km. Not bad for 4 English boys who had never attempted anything like this sort of challenge before.

After saying Adiós to Dan yesterday. We also said 'Auf Wiedersehen' to Thomas and Stefan from Germany, who were continuing on the Camino but who's projected pace was going to be slower than Jake and I could afford.

Davinia was the next to leave, she had an early bus to Barcelona as she had to be back at work Wednesday. We were all really sad to see her go, she had proved to be really good fun. Jake in particular was really going to miss her. He had formed a great friendship with her and had chatted incessantly in Spanish for the previous 3 days. She had taught Jake so much Spanish and we had definitely helped her to improve her English. Their friendship wasn't romantic, but a deeper friendship had occurred in their time together.

Jake wrote the following message in his journal in English and Spanish that night: "It was amazing to meet you Davinia and to get to know you over the last few days. Thank you very much for your help with my Spanish. "Muchas gracias por me ayudando con mi Españo."

After Davinia, we waved off the coolest Canadian we had ever met. George left us in Burgos as he went onto hike the Camino Oviedo route from the Northern coastline of Galicia. We were gutted to see him go but we wished him the best of luck. His advice had been invaluable, especially regarding finding the best short cuts, the best albergue and 21 useful things you can do with yoghurt!

The final goodbye was always going to be the hardest.

Harry left for his flight to Santander at 1:30 pm and it was safe to say I nearly flooded Burgos with my tears, even though I deliberately wore my dark sun glasses in a vain attempt to conceal my emotion. Both Jake and I said a huge thank you to Harry for coming with us and supporting us on this journey. We honestly couldn't think of anyone we would rather have done this adventure with. To walk 326 km with multiple blisters, yet also with determination, humour and laughter was a real credit to my eldest son. I was very proud of him, for everything he was previously but especially for what he had become in just those 2 weeks on Camino.

I quietly cried until we reached the outskirts of Burgos. It was a hot afternoon, but that sun could not easily dry my tears. Jake too walked in silence. He wasn't demonstrably emotional, but he too wore his sun glasses all day and they obscured what was later to be admitted, he was tearful too. I still try to rationalise those tears.

I think the Camino bonds you like no other experience and for 2 weeks we had lived, walked, ate and slept together intensively. The only thing we did separately was use the toilets … even then we frequently shared our experiences of that particular function; verbally at least!

I love all 3 of my children, there is no pecking order to my affections.

Harry has always had a touch of vulnerability about him which has always made me protective of him and enclose him with the parental defensive shield. I rarely lose my temper. My easy-going nature was only really tested throughout his childhood on the very rare occasions that Harry was treated poorly or unfairly. A red mist of protective anger could descend. The poor unfortunate who had roused the dragon in me, could subsequently suffer a verbal tirade. Harry has developed into a fine young man with a clear view of what and where he wants to end up. He will be a good catch for a life partner in the coming years I'm sure.

Typical of Harry, he suggested that he took an earlier bus to Santander airport leaving at 2 pm rather than the 4 pm bus we had originally targeted. His reasoning was simple, it gave Jake and I an extra 2 hours of time to make up for all of our lost walking time. I loved that sensitivity in his thinking.

The Harry that was returning to England, was a different Harry to the one who flew out to South Western France on 30th March 2017. I liked the changes in him very much.

Jake journaled that night: "Thanks Harry! You are not only my brother, but my best friend and I can't wait to do more crazy adventures with you. I love you so much (I saved my tears for after you'd left by the way, unlike dad!)" He also owned up, "Yes mum. When Harry left, I cried like a baby!"

Despite having lost a lot of valuable walking time waiting for Harry's bus in Burgos we were determined to make up some lost ground and time, especially as Harry's bus left in the afternoon, Jake and I were now walking in the hottest part of the day. That said, just over 20 km and 4 hours later we arrived at our albergue in Hornillos del Camino.

Preparing for the next day felt a little daunting. Ahead of us lay a test that was to be mental as much as physical.

Over the next 5 days we would be walking 'The Meseta', a high plateau stretching for 5 to 7 days, often avoided by pilgrims due to its vast unchanging landscapes that challenge even the strongest of wills. Whilst a little anxious about this unknown area, the reputation of which had been emphasized in all the guidebooks, Jake and I were ready to take on its challenge. Could we complete it, and could we regain some lost time?

Jake's final post that night on our Facebook page was to finally own up: "Yes mum. When Harry left, I cried like a baby!"

DISTANCE TRAVELLED: 336 km
DISTANCE TO SANTIAGO: 463 km

Chapter Thirteen

Wednesday 12th April 2017
Camino Day Thirteen: Hornillos del Camino
to Boadilla del Camino

This was our longest day to date, 41 km in total which we walked in about 8 hours. We left earlier than usual to avoid the heat and were rewarded with a stunning sunrise. We were determined to take on the Meseta.

We certainly missed our former team mates, but we still managed to catch up with Thomas, Stefan and Manolo. We also met many more fantastic people and were loving every second of this unique and extended experience.

We had found a new walking partner in the albergue in Hornillos Del Camino, a German student called Hannah. She was a fast walker too and it's safe to say that we struggled to keep up with her at times. She was walking fast, in part, because she had a real fear of the Meseta. I think she was as grateful to be walking with us as we were with her. We chatted all day and it was clear that in the tougher times, chatting with other pilgrims was proving a fantastic distraction to the physical and mental challenges provided by this vast and featureless section.

We blamed Hannah for both getting us up so early and for walking for so long. Her reasoning had been quite simple, get a head start on the Meseta and smash it in the first day. We had all enthusiastically signed up to this strategy last night and to the resulting 6:30 am departure. It meant we would be walking in the dark and so we at last could justify the daily transportation of our headtorches that had been so kindly sponsored by Petzl Headtorches, back in the UK.

The walk in those early hours was blissful. It was peaceful, cool and we were the only people seemingly up and about.

We made fantastic progress having walked over 12 km before breakfast. After a coffee and hot chocolate stop, we knocked off another 10 km with a well-maintained fast pace. We overtook every pilgrim we could see ahead of us.

As the Meseta is so featureless, targeting a distance in front of you is difficult, so a new unspoken strategy was instigated by our walking trio; 'See them and catch them.'

We overtook a shepherd and his flock of sheep on one particularly difficult ascent just after Astores. At the summit we enjoyed a 10 minute chat with Hersch, the first Icelander we had met on the Camino. He was a lovely, bespectacled chap, with a dramatic white beard. He was walking in quite unusual socks and sandals and was also the whitest man I have ever seen! He must have been wearing sun cream of the highest factor to maintain that pale skin. Jake and I were now as a brown as a berry in contrast and we were also using high factor lotion! I was struck once again at how often I can judge people by their appearance. Hersch may not have been walking in attire that made him the coolest looking pilgrim on Camino, but he was certainly one of the best that we ever met.

That 10-minute conversation reiterated the deep spirit of the Camino for me. It was a short chat, but somehow reached a depth that in normal living would not naturally have happened. He was struck by our reasons for walking and Jake's personal story in particular. It was a fantastic exchange and a salutary reminder to me of the need to be less judging in my preconceptions of people. The Camino, in essence was teaching me a lot personally. Not least I was learning time and time again that some of the very best people in the world can actually prove to be the most nonconformist.

We ate our lunch at Iberia de la Vega where we bought Bocadillos and coke.

Our fast pace had given us some choices: we could stay put in Iberia de la Vega and claim a 32 km walk or push on even further with an extra 9 km to reach Boadilla. We elected for the latter, despite the pain from my, by now, shrieking feet.

Taking off our boots at the end of the day was the best yet.

We were very relieved to reach the albergue by 4:50 pm, making this one of the longest walking days yet on our Camino. At the end of this long day and we were looking forward to resting up a bit and conserving our energy for the next 4 days. We were hoping to make León in a total of 5 days. All in all, despite the challenge of these 41 km and our exhaustion it had been another great day.

Jake and I washed though all of our clothes, his first experience of this chore. He too was learning things about himself in this experience. We Facetimed home and my Mum, now living at Lizzie's house in France. Life felt good.

We pondered the daunting, yet challenging and exciting prospect of an 18 km featureless stretch of the Meseta along an old Roman Road. We had this to look forward to tomorrow morning. This stretch had no water fountains, towns or cafes and was potentially the longest unsupported section on the whole of the Camino Frances.

We posted our thanks that night, for all the vocal support and encouragement we were receiving from family and friends which was proving to be a huge boost.

DISTANCE TRAVELLED: 377 km
DISTANCE TO SANTIAGO: 422 km

Chapter Fourteen

Thursday 13th April 2017
Camino Day Fourteen: Boadilla del Camin to
Carrión de los Condes

We were now two weeks into our Camino. By Day 15 we would be over halfway to Santiago! We had also completed Day 2 of the Meseta. This region is interesting. Clearly it has some sort of psychological hold on the minds of some pilgrims. Many choose to skip it, catching the bus to León and surprisingly, to me at least are still eligible to claim a completion certificate or 'Compostela' in Santiago, despite failing to walk 130 km of the 800 km total! I can understand the logic even if it would prove an anathema to me.

For me on this Camino: there is no test if there is no test!

Whilst other Pilgrims like Hannah, our German companion really did seem to dread the Meseta, I was actually starting to like it. So was Jake. Maybe the challenge element elevated our personal satisfaction levels. I was reminded that in life we often take greatest personal satisfaction from the moments that challenge us most of all.

My thinking was simple in a practical way as well. The landscape is totally flat. Therefore, we could make greater progress with our fast walking pace. Our usual walking speed was now nearly always touching 7 km an hour and we were able to apply and maintain that speed for hours at a time.

The Meseta gets very hot in the afternoon sun. Temperatures in mid-April were now touching 28 degrees by 11:30, so there was logical method in our madness of getting up early and cracking on. Our tactic was now to walk early, walk fast and arrive at our hostel where possible by 2 pm, which gave us good recovery time, washing time and an opportunity to choose the best beds in the hostel. This Moorman Boys 'Wise Pilgrim' logic was very simple on our Camino.

The respite time in the hostel was proving very important and definitely something to target. We could eat, shower (always a joy after a hot sweaty day) rest up, (Jake often took a siesta, me less so) and chat to other pilgrims. This was always enjoyable. Our 'English Boys' approach to the Meseta was again in action.

We walked for 6 km before breakfast leaving our hostel at 06:45. I'm a pretty poor sleeper, so getting up early was not too difficult, though the pending daily Camino challenge means that you have to physically and mentally make more of an effort to get yourself up. Usually by 5 am I would be awake anyway and in the next hour I would lie in bed and mentally start to plan the day. I would also start to write my daily blog at that time. It gave me some good reflection opportunities. The Camino was teaching me an awful lot about life in general.

I was up, toileted and showered by 6 am, when I woke Jake and Hannah. There were no shops in Boadilla, so breakfast had to wait till we found something. Today was to be a more relaxed 26 km after that long shift yesterday.

Another early start was rewarded with another superb sunrise over the Canal de Castilla. We made rapid progress before breakfast, walking an average of over 6 km an hour. The first 6 km to Fromista was fantastic walking. Again, we walked with headtorches on and watched the sun rise over the distant horizon. The rural community in this surreal landscape have built massive concrete water irrigation channels that run for miles in every direction and enable water to be piped many miles to the seemingly never-ending fields of maize and other crops that stretch out before the walker in every direction. Concrete sluice gates enable targeted water channelling by the farmer. The water in the irrigation channels is freezing cold, sourced from deep underground I guess, and provides a fast flowing and fantastic balm to a hot pilgrim's aching feet.

We were told that apparently, when you're hungry you can walk a whole lot faster. It seemed true to us and in the context of the featureless Meseta, that seemed to help us too.

We saw storks, finches, butterflies, heard cuckoos and woodpeckers.

We enjoyed our breakfast of coffee and croissants with Hannah as first light developed. We walked the remaining 20 km of this day's travel at a more tranquil pace. Finishing by 1 pm was a realistic target.

We met more interesting characters on Day 14, including Bill from Tennessee, USA. He was a Catholic, so, we talked religion, man-made and God-given and the importance of faith and family. He was very fit and walked well, managing to maintain a pace of about 5 kmh. That was an impressive pace at 70 years old and I made a mental note to make that speed a future target for me in 18 years' time. We also met Cathy a paediatrician from Tennessee, who was a walking buddy of Bill's, though some distance ahead of him on the trail.

We also met Will, a former student from Chicago and caught up yet again with Antonio from Brazil. We had last seen him 5 days before. We ended up enjoying a post picnic lunch with the Americans and chatted about politics. They wanted to talk Brexit and I wanted to talk Trump, so we had plenty to chat about. They were excellent companions and we had so much in common: personal values and faith. Again, the Camino was taking our conversations to a depth that would be very unusual when strangers meet back home. I guess the 'test' element of this epic walk, allows for greater freedom in people's conversations. It was so refreshing to talk about deeper things; things that really do matter rather than just the weather or the latest football results.

The Meseta is certainly a unique place- so very flat and very featureless, meaning there is literally nothing on the path to aim for. It stretches for miles ahead of you. Previously, in tougher sections of The Camino, my way of dealing with the harder challenges was to always set a visible target for myself. I had frequently reassured myself with thoughts like this: 'reach that tree on the horizon and it will be a little better.'

That strategy could not apply on the Meseta.

There was absolutely nothing to aim for.

Luckily Jake continued to boost me with his unique style of banter and humour. He journaled that night: "Please keep me in your thoughts as I don't think I can handle dad's attempt at Spanish much longer. He called multiple women 'Señor' again today!"

I would like to claim this was untrue and exaggerated, sadly, it wasn't. In truth, I was really struggling with the Spanish language, whilst totally relishing the long-distance Spanish Way of St James.

We opted to cook in the donativo hostel as it was Maundy Thursday and most restaurants were on a restricted menu and all the shops were shut. Easter is a massive time of festival in Catholic-influenced Spain. Maybe the Catholic faith is less enthusiastically practised in modern Spain now, than in years and ages gone by, but its effect on local customs and culture is still enormous. The nuns who ran the hostel, were once again unavailable for singing, dancing or cooking. I was starting to believe that the tales of 'The Singing Nuns', so prevalent amongst Camino pilgrims, were all Camino chatter with no actual substance. Or maybe their non-attendance was personal to Jake and I and they didn't actually want to perform for us! Maybe, the Camino would end for us without that unique experience, but it would be one of the key factors for me to return and do it all again in the future. Who knows? They weren't performing tonight yet again, is all I do know.

The decision to push on with some extra distance yesterday was justified as we had reached Carrión in time to get to the supermarket where we bought and lunch and dinner. Dinner was a very civilised affair and also very British, including strawberries and cream. Over dinner we chatted some more to Bill and Cathy. They were interesting people, good friends and walking partners who were both practising Christians with a strong faith. Bill was Catholic, whilst Cathy was from a more evangelical and free church background, not dissimilar to our own. They both truly believed that Donald Trump would be good for America. The timing of our walk was all the more interesting in terms of world politics. The approach to Easter 2017 had seen a year of political shocks across the Western world, America had voted in Trump, despite all the pre-election forecasts and exit polls saying this would be impossible and more recently, to my and Jake's personal consternation, Britain had just voted for 'Brexit' from the European Union. So, our conversations with our American companions had an extra dimension and were never dull.

The dinner I cooked that night, we shared with a Dutch girl named Moulou and a German traveller called Christian. They had forgotten that the shops would be shut for Easter and had no food. For them the Camino truly provided; or at least we did! We had plenty of food and a culture of sharing is totally immersed within the spirit of the Camino. We went out to watch the Maundy Thursday procession with a whole gang of pilgrims we had got to know including Betty and Diane from Ireland, Thomas from Germany who we had caught up with once again (he was the guy who had played and beat Jake at chess back at Atapuerca. In the donativo on the evening of our tenth day, Thomas had challenged Jake to a game of chess 'with a twist!' Thomas played with his back to the table and played completely from memory. He duly thrashed Jake.) We also met up with the 'Philippine' Girls.

The Procession was a traditional affair, with icons, men wearing long black capes carrying statues of Jesus and the Virgin Mary on big platforms with long carrying poles. Teams of 8 men would carry each portable shrine.

Whilst it was an interesting cultural experience it was not one that personally connected with me. I had lapsed from that form of Christianity some years previously despite my upbringing where Catholicism was a very strong influence. I still recognised the positive elements within this very Spanish culture; the way the whole town came out to participate in this important festival, was definitely something to celebrate. It was clearly still such an important part of their culture. The respectful silence was also something to witness. It was eerily quiet with thousands lined up in the streets as the procession unfolded. I wondered whether in the UK whether I would ever witness such a respectful turnout, in every town across the land, for something so obviously religious.

DISTANCE TRAVELLED: 403 km
DISTANCE TO SANTIAGO: 396 km

Chapter Fifteen

Friday 14th April 2017
*Camino Day Fifteen: Carrión de los Condes
to Sahugún*

Today we walked 2 guidebook stages in just one day, clocking up over 40 km in the process. Not a bad feat when the fearsome reputation of the Meseta is taken into account.

The Meseta was proving to be a hot region with brooding horizons and villages in the distance that seemed to be mirages. I cannot begin to understand how pilgrims manage to walk this area in the heat of summer where temperatures can hit 40 degrees or more. Fortunately for us, it never got much hotter than 28 degrees and by that time in the afternoon we would usually be near to or at our next destination.

Today was very hot. On the morning of Day 15 we left early again after a homemade breakfast of muesli and fresh milk to tackle the much feared 'Roman Road'. I walked most of it with Cathy and we talked more life, faith, politics and the similarities between her work in medicine and mine in education. It was interesting and helped us to eat up those 18 km. Hannah fell behind us and we didn't see her again during the day's walk. Her pace had dropped whilst we seemed to have regained a bit more 'Pep in our Step!' We ended up walking with Seoin from South Korea and we enjoyed a simple cafe lunch with her, before pushing on again on our own.

We chose to walk 13 km extra to get to Sahagún and probably regretted it for the majority of those 13 km as it definitely, in our view at least, won the award of 'Dump of the Camino'. But we reassured ourselves by achieving a new personal best of 42 km in a day, a distance of about 28 miles. That night, we were 2 very happy albeit tired Peregrinos.

Once again, we met more awesome people on Day 15 and definitely felt a 'thank you' was owed to Jake's Spanish teachers from North Halifax Grammar School for his newly improved ability to communicate incessantly in Spanish. Those school staff would have been very proud of him. He was chatting with ease to every Spaniard we came across and his ability to communicate in Spanish was certainly improving every day. The hostel in Sahugún was fine even if the town itself was a dive! It was very basic and a very cheap night's accommodation at 5 Euros a night each.

So far, we were very pleased with our Meseta effort. We were now walking long distances and gaining time daily on our targeted finish day in Santiago. We were now ahead of schedule and could anticipate some rest days with the girls in about 12 days. In the last 10 days we had averaged over 38,000 steps a day. Both our Phones gave similar readings on their inbuilt steps counter feature.

We were now lean, fast walking and experienced Camino Pilgrims and we were feeling pretty fit. We had the appetite of a lion and would devour vast amounts of food, but always making sure we didn't have to carry it with us. Pilgrims on the Camino obsess about saving weight just as much as they do about caring for their feet!

DISTANCE TRAVELLED: 444 km
DISTANCE TO SANTIAGO: 355 km

STEPS	
49,977	14 Apr 2017 >
35,280	13 Apr 2017 >
49,241	12 Apr 2017 >
30,143	11 Apr 2017 >
32,369	10 Apr 2017 >
30,523	9 Apr 2017 >
26,733	8 Apr 2017 >
34,480	7 Apr 2017 >
40,484	6 Apr 2017 >
33,477	5 Apr 2017 >
41,300	4 Apr 2017 >

Chapter Sixteen

Saturday 15th April 2017
Camino Day Sixteen: Sahugún to Reliegos

C R I K E Y! This is a word those of us of a certain age used back in the day. It was an excellent word to describe Day 16.

On Day 16, the Meseta gave us a final test, only 32 km of walking and 10 km less than the previous day, but it certainly tested me out! Our walk was again as flat as a pancake with the Roman Road stretching on and on and on in front of us. The surface was made of compacted round stones and it hurt!

It seemed to me that a pattern was evolving. Easier one day and harder the next. Only today it felt like the pendulum had swung still further and were now on a roll of 2 consecutive tough days.

We climbed the equivalent of only 3 flights of stairs ALL day which really is far too flat for people used to the steeply angled Pennine hills of West Yorkshire where we live. We had no villages to break the journey and only passed 3 other pilgrims in the entire day. This was really unusual because we always seemed to 'burn up' other pilgrims due to the 'Pep in our Step' first referenced to us English Boys by an American lady way back near Pamplona some 250 km and a whole lifetime ago.

Today really was a physical and mental test for me. I was never going to do a 'stop and eject' but my heels were squealing again, so, arriving in Reliegos was a real relief. My feet felt like they have been thwacked a thousand times by a wooden mallet.

I had to zone out several times this morning, listening to music from Hillsong and Life Worship, contemporary bands whose music is often played at our church. It felt a little ironic when songs with the titles of 'Even when it hurts' and 'Wide open space' came on the playlist. I had to privately giggle despite my feet saying it wasn't really very funny! At least we made it safely to Reliegos and we were now only 324 km from Santiago.

We were now positioned to make León, our 4th of the 5 principal cities of El Camino by 1 pm on Sunday and so have a chance to witness the Easter Sunday celebrations there.

We were fortunate to meet David from Pisa, a colonel in the Italian Police who we talked and walked with for the last 8 km. He really helped to distract me from the pain in my feet. He was a lovely guy, on his 3rd Camino. His wife likes walking too but for just a day at a time! So, she was staying at home with their children. I reflected on this fact and thought it sounded a familiar tale to my lovely wife Nicky.

So, whilst Day 16 was tough I reminded myself of the link with the calendar day. It was Easter Sunday and I recollected that the Easter story started off with the toughest of circumstances. I also reminded myself that my principal walking buddy, Jake was still stuck in a wheelchair on 15th April 2016. So, I had many reasons to actually be cheerful. I just trusted and hoped that my brain would convey that more positive thinking to my feet in due course!

I think perhaps, my confidence that we had tamed the Meseta had been hit by a dose of cold reality. I had found yesterday's 42 km slog to Sahagún to be relatively easy, albeit long. Travel today was long and as straight as an arrow on a dirt track constructed of round compacted stones the size of plums.

I was reminded that I'd faced similar feelings in 2005 completing the Yorkshire 3 Peaks Challenge and in 2008 when undertaking the UK National 3 Peak challenge, where you climb the 3 highest peaks in England, Scotland and Wales (Scafell, Ben Nevis and Snowden) and aim to complete the climbs and travel between them in 24 hours. In each case, as I completed the summit of the last peak; (Snowden in the National challenge and Ingleborough in the Yorkshire challenge), the elation on both occasions was almost overwhelmed by the despair I felt when I calculated that we still had a 5 mile walk from those mountains back to our vehicles.

The Meseta was similar. I had so nearly cracked it, but there was still around 40 km to go and those 40 km were going to hurt. The challenge wasn't over even though my brain thought it was.

It also felt tougher as we had Facetimed Nicky, Rosie and Harry at home during our breakfast stop. They were all still in bed, in part due to the time lapse and Harry's long journey home from Burgos. It brought home the reality that we were still being challenged physically and mentally, whilst they seemingly chilled in luxury, in their own comfortable beds. Whilst still loving the Camino I realised I was missing them badly. I was missing my wife for so many reasons and I now appreciated that our 28-year marriage counted for something much more special than I had understood pre-Camino. I saw it as a rock on a shoreline. Sometimes battered and under threat of being swept away, but never actually lost or destroyed. We had never been apart this long, and I appreciated just how much I loved her and missed her. I knew too, that I really did want to share a Camino type experience with her.

We passed though just 2 small villages in a whole day's worth of walking. We overtook a record low of just 3 Pilgrims, Joel and George from Hungary who had left separately and a good 40 minutes earlier than us and David the Italian Police colonel. We must have been walking well to overtake the Hungarian boys even if it felt otherwise.

At the albergue that afternoon Jake collapsed into my bed and slept in my sleeping bag, all the time un-showered, which in my view demonstrated a new and very shabby level of pilgrim behaviour. But I kind of understood why he did. We were shattered.

Finding food provided a new and interesting experience. Religious is a tiny hamlet and the nearest bigger village is probably 7 km further down the trail. Fortunately, it did have a 'House Supermarket.' This is exactly what it sounds like - a private house with the front room turned into a supermarket of sorts, selling a minor range of anything. So, whilst Jake snoozed, I bought the necessary ingredients from a fairly limited range to produce a 'Pasta Slop' for tea: garlic, tuna, pasta, cheese (the Spanish variety definitely not a patch on a mature cheddar), onion and sweetcorn. It was apparent that Seoin had nothing to eat, so naturally I cooked for her too. She definitely had the 'Pilgrim Appetite', devouring 2 full bowls. She was a lovely girl, a teacher who reminded me very much of Bernie my eldest niece from Birmingham; they both have the same intoxicating belly laugh.

Apparently, every other pilgrim that day seemed to have chosen the alternative route along the road to avoid the long straight compacted track we had walked. On the plus side we really enjoyed our only treat of the day: a cappuccino and a coke in a dusty and long forgotten village for just 3 Euros.

What a bargain living in Spain is proving to be.

Jake's Journal

Today was flipping hard: another long and uneventful Roman Road for about 31 km. Parts of this stage are said to resemble the Savannahs of Africa but thankfully it wasn't as hot as that due to a few well-positioned clouds. My iPod had no battery so unlike dad I couldn't listen to music. This gave me a pretty radical opportunity to think and contemplate some pretty deep stuff which was sick. I'm super thankful to be here and don't want it to end but tomorrow we reach León (our last big city before Santiago) and it's also my birthday in a week so I'm actually buzzing despite this being a tough challenge. We met more amazing people from all over the world and ate tea with Seoin - the coolest Korean around. 'Me encanta El Camino', but I miss my mum, Yorkshire and my friends a lot.

DISTANCE TRAVELLED: 475 km
DISTANCE TO SANTIAGO: 324 km

Chapter Seventeen

Sunday 16th April 2017
Camino Day Seventeen: Reliegos to León

26 km no longer seems a daunting distance to walk. We had got up early, determined to make León in good time and enjoy extra recovery time whilst witnessing the Easter Sunday celebrations.

León is a big city with a huge cathedral that is unbelievably attractive, and we were determined to make the most of it within our tight travel itinerary. We set off with 2 other pilgrims: Loudy from Catalonia, in the Basque Country of Northern Spain and Antonio from Portugal who teaches in Saudi Arabia.

This was the only time in the whole Camino Frances where we were concerned that we might be lost. As Reliegos was a spur off the main route, there were no yellow arrows or 'Way' markers apart from the very first one in the centre of the hamlet. We proceeded to walk for 6 km without a route sign or yellow arrow of any description, increasingly concerned that we may have gone significantly off-piste. A 'Wise Pilgrim' is always aware that any distance off route has to be doubled to just return to the route. We didn't like the idea of walking 12 m unnecessarily one bit. In my logic, a distant field of vivid yellow rape seemed to geographically match up with the sketchy route plan in our guidebook. Google Maps wasn't an affordable option when abroad, and therefore unavailable as back up to our Camino route finding. So, we walked in hope more than certainty. Self-doubt would have been much greater if we weren't walking alongside our 2 latest Camino companions, especially as were walking along a dark and featureless side road with no one else visible on that cold dawn morning.

Antonio and Loudy were good company, if a little slow as walkers and their conversations helped to pass the time. Jake in particular relished the chance for more Spanish practice and once again he held a conversation that went way further than a more typical stranger exchange on a dusty road in our more normal lives. The shared purpose of walking the Camino, opened up another conversation of significance, beyond the day to day mindless exchanges that we so often fall onto in our busy western lives.

My only wish that morning? I would have liked to walk faster as it was freezing cold. I had my coat, hat, gloves and long trousers on; my full array of clothing, with no spares. The slower pace meant that I never actually warmed up until we reached Manila's de Las Mulas where we returned to the main Camino route. Jake and I then broke away, making much better time. We were also hugely relieved. We hadn't actually got lost.

We took our second breakfast at a local cafe enjoying fresh croissants for 2, coffee and hot chocolate for €4.50. Wow! Another bargain.

The walk into León was not the prettiest of the last 2 weeks, pretty dull to be honest, mainly paths along main roads and through some industrial estates. But once in the old town it was impressive.

We were elated, we had completed the Meseta!

Never before has the thought of hills and undulating ground felt so attractive. I vowed there and then never to moan about the hills at home: hills which cannot be avoided on foot or by bike as I commute to work each day.

We had actually enjoyed the Meseta until yesterday. We both suffered a little, but being typical British men, we only owned up to each other afterwards! At least we can claim that we 'Manned Up': a far better and more appropriate use of that particular term by me this time around. Of course, I didn't know of his illness when I first uttered that phrase, but I can't easily use that term now, in the main, due to my eternal shame at its use first time round! So, it is cathartic to be able to use the 'Man Up' term once again without a tinge of guilt!

We enjoyed triple dollops of ice cream on the afternoon courtesy of the Philippine girls. We enjoyed the chance to take some downtime and catch up with fellow pilgrims from the Philippines, Korea, Hong Kong, Hungary and France during the afternoon. It really had started to feel like the League of Nations. We badly missed our family and friends but we were loving the international context of the Camino.

We chose to stay at an albergue allegedly run by more 'Singing Nuns'. Guess what? It was Easter Sunday and they were apparently having another day off! We were starting to take their repeated no shows personally. We had missed them every single time!

The hostel was very full, unsurprising in a sense as León is the last major city before Santiago and is the place that pilgrims who wanted to skip the Meseta restarted the route. It is also only a 1 week walk from Santiago which made it an attractive starting point for pilgrims with holiday restrictions, who wanted to ensure they still got a Compostela in Santiago.

The Camino Camaraderie made Easter Sunday 2017 feel very special. The actual walking could claim no credit on that front, as for most of the day we had walked alongside roads; our 3rd day in a row of tarmac trudging. A fair amount of all the Caminos (there are nearly 20 of them apparently) involve walking on tarmac. I'm certain that it doesn't help knee joints or bad backs and sadly I suffer a little with both.

We were more and more aware that, in just 12 days, we would meet Nicky and Rosie in Santiago at the finishing line of this trek. It is hard to express our emotions at that thought. We couldn't wait for that end in one sense as we love those girls so much and desperately wanted to see them, but then it would also mean our Camino would be over. We were tempted to consider keeping on walking! We still loved the Camino that much.

Jake's Journal

I kept falling asleep everywhere yesterday and was absolutely knackered this morning. However, we got up and left the albergue pre-sunrise and I'm so glad we did. Five minutes into the walk we met up with Antonio from Portugal and Laudy from Barcelona, Laudy didn't speak English so it was a great chance to practice some Spanish. After about an hour of chatting we got onto the subject of why we were walking the Camino. Thankfully my Spanish lived up to the task and I was able to tell her my story which resulted in her breaking down in tears in the middle of the road. It made me realise how important personal stories really are and how blessed I am to be able to help and encourage others through my own experience. It turned out she had also recently experienced the confines of a wheelchair and so within a few minutes we were able to relate to one another on a whole new level, regardless of the age, gender and nationality difference - for me, it was one of the most powerful experiences I've had so far on the Camino.

It's amazing how quickly friendships form with other pilgrims and it was radical to catch up with my favourite South-East Asians today: the Philippine Girls.

León is a cool place and we managed to get a few more stamps on our pilgrim passports. Plus; I was so hyped to see the mountains in the distance today after nothing but flat featureless walking for 5 solid days.

A special shout out to the best dad in the world for giving me the adventure of a lifetime!

Buen Camino and Happy Easter.

DISTANCE TRAVELLED: 501 km
DISTANCE TO SANTIAGO: 298 km

Chapter Eighteen

Monday 17th April 2017
Camino Day Eighteen: León to St. Martin del Camino

Always an early riser, the Camino has been no different for me. The Spanish gain of an hour has just meant I'd woken naturally around 5 am instead of the 6 am norm of the UK. It's not a bad time to be up to be honest. It means I can study and 'enjoy' at closer quarters the 'dawn chorus' of my fellow Peregrinos! Last night's hostel companions were boisterous snorers: Jake and I were surrounded by Germans in Leon - they get my vote for the loudest snorers on the Camino so far.

We always knew that the early morning was going to be interesting in this, the first busy hostel that we have stayed in. Our full dorm of 36+ beds has just 3 showers and 2 toilets. The Queen song 'Under Pressure' sprang to mind as I avoided the morning rush by getting in early.

The 'joy' of getting up early meant I avoided 'Operation Stack' with the toilets, never a nice experience especially when our fellow travellers see that there is no toilet roll left. I was mildly amused by the thought and would have liked to be a fly on the wall at that particular realisation point? Actually, on instant reflection I certainly didn't want to be a fly on the wall anywhere near those two toilets. I did concede though that I definitely would like to give a penny for the thoughts of the poor half-awake seated pilgrim who learnt (far too late) that this hostel had suddenly gone paperless!

The toilet roll was already on its last legs at 5 am.

Jake and I appear to be rarities in these parts because we like to be clean pilgrims and shower both morning and evening.

Today SHOULD be an easy 21 km but my illustrious sidekick had informed me at bedtime that there's an add on we could do today which reduces the add on we would need to do tomorrow. As I prepared to wake my 'Reason for my Camino', I began preparing myself for a 30 km stretch rather than the more attractive 24 km I had anticipated. So be it. El Camino is never scripted!

We left the hostel after a basic breakfast of bread and jam at 07:45. We made decent progress through downtown León and reached La Virgin del Camino within 2 hours where we stopped for a proper second breakfast. As usual we Facetimed Nicky who was just waking up back in Halifax.

Jake ordered a 'Limonade de León', which rather than the expected lemonade turned out to be a large glass of very strong and very potent Sangria. Whilst 9 am was a little too early for me to be drinking alcohol it seemed to invigorate Jake. He had his best day of walking since we started the Camino! The Sangria also seemed to convince him that taking the alternative route to our next stopover was a good idea. This 'alternative route' would add 6 km today but save 6 km tomorrow. I confess that I was happy to support his decision. The walking on the alternative route was still a bit dull, but I zoned out for an hour or so listening to music and as we touched a speed of 7 km an hour for 2 hours, we soon ate those up. The day went well I actually exaggerated the distance we covered: we had walked just 28 km, leaving a little over 20 km to walk tomorrow to Astorga.

As we walked along the main road, we played a favourite game of ours 'Pilgrim Catch up.' We overtook a lot of people and were walking fast, a clear 7 kmh for 2 hours. We caught up again with Jay, a retired American Art teacher who was struggling a little with some nasty blisters, I provided some plasters as relief which he really did appreciate.

Jay was easy to chat to as we lunched together outside a small and basic grocery shop in a very small village. It was warm and sitting eating baguettes filled with cheese, onions and tomatoes was proving to be a very enjoyable daily occurrence. We left him again on the route into St Martin del Camino, only to meet up again at the nights hostel where I added his laundry to be machine washed with ours and he bought us a beer in return. Sharing and generosity are a real theme of The Camino.

Jake and I sauntered down to a small supermarket where we bought a packet of breakfast cereal for tomorrow morning and chorizo, yoghurt and wine for this evening. We had been invited to eat with Bart from Holland and Keith from Ireland who were now walking the whole Camino together (both of whom we'd met on Day 1 at Roncesvalles in the Pyrenees), along with the

Hungarian Boys: Joel, George and Gabor. They were all staying in a hostel 100 metres up the road.

We dropped of our contribution to the meal before returning to our hostel for a siesta and to Facetime Nicky, Jake's grandma Jenny, and Jon and Tracey, friends from home. Tracey is a senior Governor at my school.

We enjoyed great fun over a shared meal, simple and yet so tasty. Everyone contributed a bit. We ate spaghetti, chorizo and vegetables; bread with a garlic dip, and yoghurt for pudding washed down with a local red with the deepest dinge in Spain. I remembered that Fred, a retired teacher from my school, had always claimed to me that the deeper the dinge (the indentation at the bottom of wine bottle) the better the wine quality. This certainly appeared to be the case today as we drank our classy yet cheap red.

St Martin del Camino was as classy as its name clearly suggests!

The International Supper was a big hit. The spirit of the Camino was so evident and every one of us had a clear personal reason for walking it.

It was over that meal that I first heard the term "Everyone has a reason for doing the Camino." So simply put but true, I think.

I have yet to meet a pilgrim who is doing the Camino because they fancied a walk or because they wanted to get personally fitter.

Every one of the Peregrinos I have met seems to have a deeper and more personal reason. Some won't share their 'Why'. Maybe it contains too raw an emotion for them to express yet. Some do. Many are walking for a loved one; many a lost loved one or one who's life hangs in the balance.

Our cause was no secret; we walked with thankfulness on two fronts: firstly, for the miracle of Jake's treatment and recovery and the way he has been allowed to re-embrace all elements of normal life in the last 12 months. Secondly, we walked for the practical opportunity through our efforts to payback for the magnificent medical treatment he had received in the last 3 years. Jake was the recipient of easily in excess of several hundred thousand pounds worth of lifesaving treatment. When people slate the National Health Service in the UK I can't agree. The surgical treatment and operative care Jake got was exemplary.

We had now already attracted over £11,000 of incredible financial support for the research and development work undertaken by the Neurological team at Leeds. Out of a tough situation some good had started to come.

Every time Jake's story was told the reaction was totally positive and supportive. We've had tears, financial sponsorship, social media posts and messages and great encouragement. Today after hearing Jake's story I was told separately by 2 pilgrims, "That's the best reason I ever heard for doing the Camino." The wording used in each verbal exchange was exactly the same.

I suppose the reality is, you need something personal to drive you to want to do the Camino. Otherwise it would be totally illogical; in reality who would want to spend 3 days in a row (like we have just done), walking roadside in the main, across 80+ km of Spanish suburbs, towns and countryside? The whole thing is nuts, but all the more special because of it. So, yes, everyone has a reason for walking the Camino!

The highlight of our day was definitely the opportunity to immerse our feet into the freezing waters of the irrigation ditch that ran through the hostel gardens. It was ice cold and sheer bliss for our battered feet. We stood there for 10 minutes in bone achingly cold and fast flowing mountain water: wow what a sensation. All the while we were observed by 5 chickens who were stood just 60 cm away from us! We could read their minds, 'These English Boys are nuts!' I think we are.

Over the past few days as we've walked, we've focused on a specific group of people in our lives and offered up thanks for their influence and support. On our first day of committing to this we thought of our immediate family Nicky, Harry and Rosie and Nicky's Mum, Jenny. Then it was the students past and present at Ravenscliffe.

Yesterday it was Jake's Academy course mates in Bradford this year. Today it was the leadership team at our Church in Bradford. They are awesome people who deliver positive, life affirming messages every week and practise a 'love your neighbour' mentality every day. I too work as a leader albeit in a secular organisation at my school. These people are seriously top of the range leaders! Today they were all in our thoughts.

So were some key extras: special families who have become great friends to us: people like the Harris, Karitons and Robinson families. We wanted to emphasise our thanks for the great support given us as a family in the last 2 years, especially when the chips were down, and Jake was so dangerously ill.

Jake's Journal

I had a great start to the day when I ordered a 'Limonade natural de León' at our first town. This turned out to be a very strong wine with a drop of lemon in it but as we'd already paid, I thought it'd be wrong to waste it, despite the fact that it was only 9 am.

Looking back, I think my early morning beverage gave me just what I needed as we then paced out the next 20 km. It was easy walking but not the greatest fun as we were simply following a main road all day. Nevertheless, I loved it. Again, I was provided with loads of time to think as well as talk to more amazing people! A bunch of our Camino friends are taking rest days in León today but I'm glad we pushed on.

It means we are 28 km closer to seeing mama and Rosie in Santiago.

Buen Camino

DISTANCE TRAVELLED: 529 km
DISTANCE TO SANTIAGO: 270 km

Chapter Nineteen

Tuesday 18th April 2017
Camino Day Nineteen: St. Martin del Camino
to Astorga

This was more like it. After 3 days of roadside toil we enjoyed a wonderful walk after the first 5 km today.

Those first 5 km were fine actually. Though on tarmac, we polished them off in about 45 minutes and I think we were probably still half asleep, so the tarmac didn't unduly bother us.

Jake hadn't been keen to get up this morning, I think 3 glasses of strong red wine for the boy who rarely drinks had acted as a sedative. Despite this we were still up and walking by 7:40 am with a slightly unconventional mini breakfast of muesli bars and fresh milk inside us.

Jay gratefully took my penultimate blister plaster. His blisters were bleeding badly, and his need was clearly greater than mine. Ironically, an hour later I found a still wrapped but discarded compeed pack on the trail, with one untouched plaster patch still inside it. The Camino was providing yet again!

Today we experienced at first hand the most pointless bridge ever built. The bridge I refer to is an impressive looking steel structure, made up of long sweeping zigs and zags and is sited about 2 km before you reach the town centre and the end of our Camino stage 20 in Astorga. The bridge is a bright green colour and towers high above the single rail track it crosses.

The information board on that bridge proudly celebrates that it was funded by the European Union. It must have cost a million euros to build at the very least. We followed the herd of pilgrims ahead of us and walked up and down all those long zig zag elevations. The bridge itself must have added at least 1 km to our walk. It was colossal. It crosses a single use, rusting rail track below and we chose to take a minute's rest at the point where the bridge crosses the track. As we stopped and caught our breath, we noticed a local man walking along the Camino route towards the bridge. However, as he got nearer the bridge, he suddenly veered off the main path, deliberately ignoring the right turn that signposted the walker to walk onto the first of the bridge's many zigzags. He calmly approached the rail track and proceeded to cross it, sauntering off towards the centre of Astorga, now a full 10 minutes ahead of us. We were flabbergasted. What a pointless bridge.

I was struck at how often do we do things that are totally pointless, just because we are told we have to or because we have always done them that way? I resolved there and then that I would always try to avoid the unnecessary and pointless in my life.

Jake and I were intentional in our walking today and we prayed as we plodded. Today we remembered friends from our church in Bradford who all live locally in Halifax. We meet up regularly, we back each other and we try to support each other.

We also focused on the young people we know; friends of Jake. Young people in Britain seem to face so much pressure in our modern, fast paced society. The young people Jake has befriended at church carry a passion for being real with their faith, something refreshing to see.

On the trail, we made good progress and once again caught up with Jay who had left much earlier than us. We also met a lady called Valerie from West Virginia USA who had tragically lost her 24-year-old daughter to cancer in 2016.

I could offer Valerie no glib or trite answers as explanation for her loss. I just expressed a hope that walking the Camino would help her to process her loss. I pondered long and hard today on our chance meeting; why had she suffered loss and I had been given a reprieve with Jake. I guess life is often unfair. We have to accept that and just try to deal with the circumstances we face. Interestingly, like me, Valerie was finding this very long walk helpful. She was walking differently, preferring to choose Casa Rural accommodation to stay in; similar to bed and breakfast and a definite step up in luxury from our hostel experience. Her husband was also a keen walker but was back home in the States. The Camino wasn't for him, but he had supported her in her desire to walk it as she struggled to come to terms with her loss.

I also spoke to Tony from school today, dealing with his own devastating loss of his wife who had died a week earlier. He's a top guy. The best accolade I can give him, is that he is 'salt of the earth' hardworking, loyal and genuine. We definitely walked the Camino for him today.

We caught up with the Hungarian Boys in Astorga and ate with them at lunchtime.

Then I took Jake off for a treat at the 5* Hotel Astorga spa. We loved it. It gave our bodies and our feet a refresh and emotionally revitalised us both.

Today we passed the 'Hobbling Pilgrim' as we approached Astorga, he still had 45 minutes or so to walk and every step looked like purgatory!

Typically, the walk in to the destination town on Camino is never easy. Astorga was several kilometres away in the distance and as ever it had felt tantalizingly close and yet still a seemingly never-ending trudge to reach.

We bumped into him later in the spa, he was called Jem and from Luxembourg (our first Luxembourger on this trip). His feet were wrecked, much worse than Jay's. He was hoping to allow them some recovery by breaking his Camino in Astorga for a second day. I was not convinced that this would work. His feet were really messed up and looked like they would need at least 2 weeks of no walking in order to recover, but it was still great to chat to him. His wife was flying out for a week in 2 days' time and they hoped to then make Santiago within 7 days, I suspected he would have to use public transport to make that liaison. His walking style and pace was all over the place. I doubted if he could even manage a walking pace of 2 km an hour.

His story reminded me of the link between a Peregrinos feet and our own families. Our feet can often be worn, blistered, bruised and hurting; so, can our family relationships. Just like we need feet to walk, so we really do need our families to try to successfully walk through the tests of life. We have to take care of our feet in order to walk well: in the same way we have to take care of family relationships. They need care and protection.

We counted our blessings that whilst sore in places, our feet were doing ok.

We ate pizza in the main square in Astorga. It was warm enough to sit outside and there was a real vibe to this pretty little town on a hill. I was somewhat bemused therefore to witness the most peaceful protest march I have ever seen. It seemed to be linked to equal rights for women. An announcement was made, followed by a minute of silence and then a contingent of female protestors stood quietly in the main square for a short while. It was done and dusted within 20 minutes of starting. The only time it ever got loud was when the town hall bell rang at 8 pm. It was all slightly surreal.

We stayed in a great albergue, sharing a side room with 8 Pilgrims. We seem to have formed a new 'Band of Brothers': Ivan, Keith, Bart, the 3 Hungarian Boys and a chap called Bernard from Birmingham. Jake called them

'The International Snorers': he was right! On the plus side, there was no farting, swearing or burping. I've found I can handle stranger's snoring well ....I just contribute my own.

Jake's Journal

The past 24 hours have been unbelievable.

Last night was so much fun, as we ate Pizza with some of the coolest guys and had a right laugh. Unfortunately, this made it a little tougher getting up this morning. Dad 'kicked off' because I wasn't ready until 7:26 rather than 7:20 am.

Regardless, we set off eventually and crossed the longest bridge on the Camino; a 130 metre Roman Bridge in Hospital De Orbigo. We decided to walk a slightly longer alternative route today to avoid the road and it turned out to be the best decision, hills, fields and forests are so underrated. We also had a banging view of the snow-capped Montes de León up ahead.

I definitely want to second what dad said about the reasons people have for doing the Camino. Every day to me is a reminder of how blessed I am to be here, not simply alive but actually living. I'm so thankful to be here. Dad offered me a night in a hotel tonight and I'm happy to say my answer was 'I'd prefer the albergue with the guys please.' This was just another example of how quickly bonds form out here.

The space to just 'be' is incredible and I'm definitely going to miss this when we arrive in Santiago in less than 10 days' time.

DISTANCE TRAVELLED: 554 km
DISTANCE TO SANTIAGO: 245 km

Chapter Twenty

Wednesday 19th April 2017
Camino Day Twenty: Astorga to Foncebadon

Day 20 was one of our best days yet. In terms of walking quality, it equalled some of the early days around the start of the Camino in St Jean, or at Arre and Logrono

Our walk was purposeful but leisurely. I was up as usual at 05:30 and woke Jake at 7 am after having already written my journal. It is weird how this journey had brought out the desire for me to write every day. I've often thought about scribing the daily happenings within my school environment. They are often very funny and, in my school, at least, we do seem to laugh a lot. But I've always resisted writing about what is such a small, personal and interconnected world.

We ate a whole packet of cornflakes between us for first breakfast and were on the trail by 07:35. We seem to eat a lot on the Camino because 12 km later by 09.30 we were onto second breakfast and by noon, we were stopping in Rabanal for a bread and cheese lunch with 8 hard-boiled eggs. I managed 6 of them, a feat only bettered in my memory Steve McQueen in the film 'Cool Hand Luke.' I seem to recall that he ate 50.

This Camino experience was developing me every day.

Today we focused on our family as we walked, which given there are 70+ on both sides of the Moorman family, meant the list was a long one. I have a great family. Like all families, we can drive each other mad from time to time but at the core there is love, respect and affection in all quarters. My parents are in their later years and have ever increasing health issues. Their wellbeing is an ongoing concern. My siblings have worked hard and have all rallied around to practically support them to find and establish a plan that keeps them happy, safe and secure and still enjoying life with a degree of independence and dignity as they zone into their late 80's and early 90's.

My brother and sisters and their families are super special to me, that recognition came about more than ever in May 2014 at the time of Jake's first operation when their unconditional love and support was so apparent. We have great nephews, nieces, cousins, aunts and uncles galore!

They are an eclectic mix of teachers, doctors, nurses and health workers, photographers, salesmen, security officers, personal assistants, classroom support staff, midwives, top secret aeronautical engineers, church pastors, financial managers and bursars, retired and current police officers, engineers, actuaries, geologists, future London cabbies, textile, fashion and design students, chemists, social workers, and even a world champion Poker player (you can google Chris Moorman if you wish!)

What I remembered and what the 'Camino family experience' over the first 3 weeks of this trip and my chat with Jem had re-taught me is that you don't choose your family, but you do choose how you behave with, interact with and treat your family.

So, day 20 of our Camino was a 'Family Shout Out' day. We had rooted for them all by the time we finished this afternoon and named every single one of them. I knew that I loved and appreciated them all and prayed that they would all proceed to have fulfilled and purposeful lives. So, in an effort to be 'Tolkienesque' in naming the families I wrote the whole list: Fowler, Moorman, Smith, Murphy, Whittaker, Maher, Jones, Gregson, Dobson, McCormick, Biggs, Ivko, Evans, Bryant, Stebbings, Bailey, Bryant, Ball, Hopwood and Adler in recognition of Michael who was due to marry Felicity my niece, in early May, in just two weeks. There was also Will 'The Beard' who is due to become my son in law in May 2019. We appreciated them all.

My one encouragement to anyone facing relationship difficulties with members of their family is to do something positive to repair and develop it. Don't wait and then ultimately regret the waiting; make contact, phone or text them and make it a 'Nike Moment - Just Do It! If it doesn't work first time, try again and again! In my experience the effort to try again, is always worth it.

After leaving the Meseta we had travelled for nearly 3 days always within a couple of hundred metres of the main road. It wasn't especially inspiring, but the Camino experience means that you often find quite bland things interesting. So, whilst I never hated the companion of the highway, I was relieved to get back onto meandering forest trails that led across pasturelands either lush green or freshly ploughed, ready for the summer growing season. Apparently, the trail would now get very pretty all the way to Santiago. I remember thinking what a 'jammy beggar' I was to be doing this with Jake, having shared the first 11 days with Harry and Dan and then meeting Nicky and Rosie at the end in Santiago. I guess I just love my family to bits, and it is radically special to be able to do this with them all.

Our donativo hostel was located on a hill, at an elevated altitude, just 2 km below the summit at Cruz de Ferro, and was freezing cold. We played 'Spoons' with our Camino Crew; a silly card game where you try to knock the other players out. I'm rubbish at it and was regularly one of the first to be knocked out. The wood burner was on and as we played, I finally started to feel toasty warm.

Jake reckoned that night that I should take the staff from my school on a Camino!

The hostel meal was good, but I was in bed by 9 pm as I was totally shattered, and it was very cold in that hostel once away from the wood burner. Today we completed 28 km of walking, tomorrow we planned to be up and out for the sunrise.

Jake's Journal

'Woahhhh' I flipping love mountains. Today was definitely a contender for our most beautiful walk so far. We had a great night last night in Astorga and I slept really well (despite international snoring, way better than a 5* hotel).

As dad has said, we've been walking for different groups of people every day and today it was the turn of our wider family.

For me my family are insanely important; no surprise considering a large percentage of my best friends are actually related to me (Harry, my cousins Joey, Isaac and Zach get a special shout out). I love all my family and I'm so blessed to have such an awesome group of people to support me. Today made me realise that I do really miss so many of them and can't wait to see them again, but more importantly it was just great to pause and be thankful for my gang.

Family is such a unique concept and I think we can all take it for granted, so taking time to think of them all, has just made me super aware of how much I owe them. After 30,000+ steps I just wanted to say how much I love and miss you.

On the subject of family, tonight we are sharing a donativo albergue with the 'League of Nations' and we'll all be eating together once again. I don't necessarily share much in common with my Camino family, other than the fact that every day we walk for hours and endure some pretty tough times together, but I'm super thankful to have met them as well. The bond is strong, and I pray the Camino provides each of them with whatever they are searching for.

Tomorrow we are aiming to get up before dawn and reach the summit of the Cruz de Ferro for the sunrise. This will undoubtedly be a super special moment and I cannot wait. Fingers crossed I'm not too tired in the morning.

DISTANCE TRAVELLED: 580 km
DISTANCE TO SANTIAGO: 219 km

Chapter Twenty-One

Thursday 20th April 2017
Camino Day Twenty-One: Foncebadon to
Ponferreda

We had an early start today as we wanted to witness the sunrise at the shrine on the summit, which meant a 6.45 am departure from the hostel. It was going to be chilly I suspected, as well as a really exciting experience.

Early this morning we passed a sign that said 216 km to Santiago. A couple of kilometres later we passed another that said 208 km. As ever there seems to be some discrepancy with Spanish signage and distance calculations. What is certain, is that by the time we roll up in Santiago, Jake and I would be able to sing with full conviction the words of the famous Proclaimers hit 'I will walk 500 Miles!'

I had woken up early again on Day 21. Yet again my sleep hadn't been great, but that had been my experience for quite a few years now and I seem to do okay with it. Margaret Thatcher the famous (or infamous, depending on your stance) British Prime Minister in the 1980's, was renowned for thriving on 4 hours sleep a night.

The pressure was now off us. We were on target to arrive in Santiago on or around 27th April 2017. We had gained on the guidebook schedules. We no longer needed to walk over 30 km a day to stay on course.

My only remaining concern on the Camino before we finish, was will I be able to find a suitable spot for Jake to get his wild camp?

We got some fantastic photos of ourselves with our Camino friends silhouetted against the sunrise.

The Cruz de Ferro was an intense emotional experience, more so because I spent the moments of sunrise there alone with Jake.

We laid our 'Burden Stones' from the Meseta at the feet of the simple pole with a cross on top. Over the last thousand years, Pilgrims have traditionally carried a stone, to represent the burdens of life that affect them. They have laid them at the shrine on Cruz de Ferro.

We placed our stones on the huge pile of rubble at the shrine at sunrise at 7:15 am. Most pilgrims bring a stone from home and carry them along the Camino. Some of the stones are huge. The pragmatist in me rejected that idea from the very outset, my pack was heavy enough thank you. Besides one of my best friends Pete had emotionally scarred me with the very concept of stone carrying. Back in 2013 I think, on a long winter walk in the English Lake District, he sneaked a huge boulder into my rucksack when I wasn't looking and I ended up carrying it unwittingly for 5+ hours, uphill and down dale!

No way was I bringing a heavy piece of stone from Yorkshire on our Camino. Besides Ryanair, our budget airline out of Stansted, wouldn't have allowed it I'm sure.

Some of the burden stones at Cruz de Ferro were enormous. Mine when I eventually chose it, was the size of a €1 coin.

I had actually changed my mind about carrying a stone myself half way through the trip.
Both Jake and I had eventually chosen a stone on the 18 km Meseta Roman Road a week ago. It was the day my heels were really bruised and screamed at me to stop walking. We both found it very tough. Thankfully I ignored my heels and Jake suffered in silence as well. It seemed right that as I was actually going to place a stone, then it should be one I carried from the toughest part of the Camino.

I placed my stone at the shrine and when doing so I symbolically placed some relationships that haven't worked out as well as I would have wished and some situations where I wish there had been a better outcome. I focused on the half dozen or so times in my 30 years of teaching that where despite my best intention's things didn't work out well. In those situations, I sought no fallout, but still it happened.

I realised that I cannot influence other people's thoughts and actions, but I can take control of my own.

I never sought or desired fall out (other people sometimes do, and it is very apparent that they enjoy it). If I had hurt people by my thoughts or actions, it had never been my intention.

On Day 21 I placed my stone symbolically to 'ditch my own baggage.' It was a liberating moment.

On the previous evening we had met Juan, a Spanish pilgrim, on his 28th continuous Camino. I was very taken with Juan. He had already walked from France to Santiago 28 times! I guessed he was a professional Camino-ite. I was reminded of just how much useless clutter we choose carry in our daily lives. Juan carried just one small rucksack, his most prized possession was his dog. It struck me that he had very little baggage to ditch, he said the Camino was his family. I was struck that in life we carry way too much physical and emotional stuff with us. This Camino was teaching me that I don't need much physically to live well and that I also have choices and ownership on what I choose to carry emotionally.

'Ditching our Baggage' can be totally liberating!

The walk across the tops and then down into the valley towards Ponferrada was lovely. To either side of the trail, were clusters of wild flowers: pinks, purples, yellows, whites and blues. Simple and beautiful in their simplicity. Sadly, we saw large forest fires on the other side of the valley and the palls of smoke hung in the damp mid-morning air. It was only April and the forest fires were already a major issue in this region.

Day 21 was a stunner, although tough at the end as we added a few kilometres at a junction just 4 km from

Ponferrada to avoid trudging along the road. If we had stuck to the road, we would have arrived 30 minutes earlier, but just as Frodo cautions in the Lord of the Rings, I'm always keen to 'get off the road!'

At the albergue I cooked a soup with vegetables, chorizo, tiny bits of bacon, (called 'Speck' by the Dutch) and frankfurter sausages. We cooked a huge pot full and then proceeded to feed half of the hostel. Other pilgrims also shared their own cooking. We washed our sausage soup down with garlic mushrooms, risotto and a Taiwanese stir fry. We were stuffed.

Our walk of 28 kilometres was awesome. We had now cleared 600 km and were feeling pretty good. I was still loving it!

Jake's Journal

Today saw my highlight of the Camino so far.

We set off at 6:45 to catch the sunrise at Cruz de Ferro - the highest point on the whole Camino.

Words cannot do justice to just how beautiful this moment was for me. Aside from the amazing sunrise, the place itself moved me. For thousands of years pilgrims have placed a stone at the foot of the Cruz, the mound of stones now is quite a sight! As I looked at the mound of stones and rocks, I was again reminded of the countless people who had sacrificed and endured to

188

make that journey and the significance of each rock present.

As many of you know the initial reason for undertaking this challenge came from a place of total thankfulness- between the ages of 16-18 I had cheated death not once but twice and so as I laid down my stone, I was reminded just how blessed I was to be here. Each of the 30,000+ steps that followed on today I counted as a blessing.

One year ago, I could barely walk.

DISTANCE TRAVELLED: 606 km
DISTANCE TO SANTIAGO: 192 km

Chapter Twenty-Two

Friday 21st April 2017
Camino Day Twenty-Two: Ponferreda to Trabadelo

We walked really well on Day 22: a total of 37 km.

We were out and walking by 7.20 am intending to do a 26 km guidebook stage, but also with our eyes on another extra 11 km on the 'Camino Dura' or 'The Hard Way.'

We swapped encouragement in our walk out of Ponferrada with some other Peregrinos: Geoff and Joanne from Texas and then met up with 2 girls from Boston USA, Molly and Kendra who were cousins. The girls, Jake and I encouraged each other to take on 'The Hard Way' and it certainly was hard but so rewarding, it really was a stunning walk over a steep sided mountain. As ever the easy conversations with Molly and Kendra kept us going, it was as if we had known each other for years. They used our conversation to get them over that mountain just as much as we used theirs for the same purpose. My heels were hurting again and the blister on my left heel was quite pronounced, but the extra kilometres of the hard way were definitely was still worth doing.

The hillside was a splash of colour: the gorse, lavender and heather were stunning.

With only a 20 km day ahead of us we planned to eat out together, with Ivan, Keith and Bart; though with Jake in attendance I was never sure when he was going to pipe up with "Why don't we do this extra...."

On Day 22, I thought about the people I work with. These are people involved with or employed like me, by Calderdale Council. The Council's strap line is: 'Everybody Different. Everybody Matters.

This Camino it has become much more than a 4 word strapline to me.

When I refer to the CMBC slogan I'm now hugely influenced by the reality that we definitely do all have far more to unite us than to divide us. On this little trudge we had met, walked, eaten, joked, sung, texted, filmed and cooked with Slavs, Italians, Hungarians, Spaniards, French, Americans, Irish, Canadians, Dutch, Austrians, Peruvians, Aussies, Danes, Icelandic's, Poles, Czechs, Brazilians, Welsh, Philippines, Koreans, Hong Kong Chinese, Taiwanese, Japanese - I could go on and on. I loved meeting them all and was all the richer for the experience of having done so. There were people on this trip who we will meet up with again and who will be dropping into Halifax in the future I'm sure.

Without dredging up old Brexit ground (I do believe we just have to get on with it now and make it work to be the best it can be) I have been so reassured to see decency, respect and compassion as the standard currency amongst all nationalities on the Camino. People shared what they had. Today, I cooked a chorizo and vegetable stew. We had far too much. About 8 people came and ate some and then proceeded to insist that we tried their Hungarian Goulash, French Risotto with

Champignons and Taiwanese stir fry. I can pack it away like the best of them but tonight, I was totally stuffed.

Cutting to my point, I heard a lot of nationalistic rubbish spouted over the last year, the fact is, that in every human being I believe there is a capacity to do good and be good. The 'Brotherhood of Man' spirit (without sounding trite) is alive and kicking on the Camino. Maybe that is why Juan, who I mentioned yesterday is walking his 28th 'there and back Camino' or why there is apparently a pilgrim who has been on Camino for over 5 years and he has now got over 7 metres of stamps in his Pilgrim Passport or 'Credential.' In a world where man still has the capacity to do great harm to his fellow man, I have found the Camino to be so uplifting because of the random acts of kindness that are witnessed every day irrespective of race, creed or colour.

We had been filming our experiences with a Go Pro and every day we asked a fellow pilgrim to do a brief introduction in their own language to our next stage. Harry had the dubious pleasure of putting this all together in an edited film once he finishes university in June 2017. How he was going to understand and translate what they have said is beyond me as we had now met someone on the Camino from countries representing 22 of the 26 letters of the alphabet. We were now left looking for a Z, Y Q and X, though I wasn't so sure that the last one was possible. Perhaps we can claim 'Y' as 'YANKS' although rather tenuous we did do a hard extra 12 km today with Kendra and Molly from the

USA and it must therefore count! They were fabulous company. Thanks again ladies; for getting us up and over the alternative 'Camino Dura'.

The challenge for Jake and me as we started to think of our return to life at home was to ensure we carry the Spirit of the Camino into our everyday lives. Engulf villages and towns with that spirit and we would indeed live in a super special world.

Back to Calderdale Council. 'We walked' the Camino for the officers, the Councillors and MPs of Calderdale on Day 22. We recognised that these remain challenging times for those serving in Local Authorities.

We ate as a group of friends again tonight and were joined by an Australian. He had swapped some banter at first; the usual cricket related stuff, but then he started to touch on the delicate issue of immigration. Fortunately, he backed off the subject when an awkward silence descended. He was quite apologetic at the end of the evening and as I learned more of his personal story.

I was again reminded that we all have our own baggage.

37 km walked. We had just 155 km left before we would reach Santiago.

I guess we wanted to see the girls!

Jake's Journal

Another 24 hours, another 30-odd km, walked, we met more awesome people, saw more awesome things and all in all just had a radical day.

I slept so well last night. We shared a room with two of the most considerate Spaniards I've met and thankfully the snoring was minimal (apart from the odd snort that dad let out, just to remind us of his presence).

After I was overwhelmed with thankfulness yesterday for my miraculous health journey, today I was keen to remember/think of/pray for all the people in my life who are still struggling with their health.

Today we had a choice between taking two routes to our destination, one was shorter, along the valley floor, the other went up over the tops. We opted for the latter route, The Camino Dura. I'm so glad we did this, our effort up some pretty steep hills was more than rewarded with the views we got at the top. It just goes to show that the harder journeys are, almost always, they prove to be the most rewarding. I definitely think this analogy applies not only when walking through Northern Spain but to life as well. Without sounding like a broken record, my hardest journey has certainly been the most rewarding.

One year ago, today (the day before my 18th birthday) I was given the greatest birthday present when I was given the 'all clear' by my doctor. I don't think I'd ever heard words that meant as much as those. One year on, the day before I turn 19, I'm still so thankful for the outcome I received, and I hope everyone I thought of today receives the same good news that I did.

DISTANCE TRAVELLED: 643 km
DISTANCE TO SANTIAGO: 155 km

Chapter Twenty-Three

Saturday 22nd April 2017
Camino Day Twenty-Three: Trabadelo to O'Cebreiro

Camino Day 23 was Jake's 19th birthday!

To celebrate, I posted a very early birthday message for him. 'King of the Mountains' - Jake Moorman. Happy Birthday! Why don't we do something special? Maybe we could go for a walk?

Our tactics had paid off and on day 23 we enjoyed the luxury of just a 21 km day albeit with 680 metres of up; on Jake's 19th birthday. I knew how to treat my boy!

Just thinking about life with Jake for a moment: I love that boy to bits, but I did hold him mainly and significantly responsible for my recent development of a few grey hairs. However, I got the best possible good morning today from a South African gentleman (the first pilgrim we had met from South Africa on our Camino) who reckoned Jake and I must be brothers! RESULT!

Jake had a brilliant birthday made very special in the simplest of ways, thanks in the main to 5 brilliant people: an Irishman, Frenchman, Dutchman and 2 fantastic American ladies. We all enjoyed a great walk and great day.

Last night we shared a room again with Keith and Bart. We were now very comfortable with each other's company. Yet again I slept badly even wishing Jake happy birthday with that Instagram message at 02:39.

It was therefore ironic that we then all overslept! I woke everyone at 07.09 and we all had breakfast, showers and still left at 08.10.

We all walked well, even catching and overtaking 'Mad' Max' who had cooked us garlic mushrooms a few days earlier when we'd shared a communal meal.

We did our usual thing with our 'Camino Comrades' and took a second breakfast complete with a birthday cake for Jake, complete with a candle, sorted by Max our newly found fast walking amigo from Toulouse.

We sang Happy Birthday to him along with his mum (via FaceTime). We then walked for another 30 minutes to a stop where we could actually design our own ink stamp for our Pilgrim Passport (Credential). Then started our 680 metre ascent to O'Cebreiro. The scenery and weather were stunning and whilst we did sweat as we climbed, it was never uncomfortable.

We completed the day's walk at 12:15 pm, taking only 4 hours to walk 21 km with all that ascent as well. We were walking well.

After lunch we all chilled together playing cards eventually eating together in the evening with a Canadian, an Italian and Antonio from Brazil who had caught up with us once again. The local forest fires made seeing the sunset impossible.

We had a fantastic evening with our Camino friends and stayed as a group of 6. The hostel which was packed solid, was surprisingly quiet overnight, a nice hostel but far too busy. The bunks were crammed together, and it felt quite weird sleeping barely 18 inches away from Molly. Don't worry Nicky! Nothing happened and there was no desire for anything to happen! We are both happily married. This was just hostel living but as I have faithfully slept next to the same woman for nearly 30 years, it felt weird.

Jake and I decided that tomorrow we would push on, a shame in one sense as our group were so well bonded, but Nicky and Rosie felt very close now.

Our football team Bristol City won 3-2 to all but secure their status in the English football Championship division. That result on Jake's birthday, and its significance all but rounded off the perfect day.

Today we climbed our last big mountain before Santiago. The climb was long, steep and hot; the equivalent of climbing Pike O' Bliscoe in the English Lake District, or Ingleborough in the Yorkshire Dales.

I'd been thinking a lot about mountains since we left the Meseta and reacquainted ourselves with undulation. I was struck that life is full of mountains; it would after all be pretty dull if it was always flat like the Meseta.

Mountains are physical obstacles to a new and sometimes better destination. You have to do the hard slog in order to get to the other side. I was very mindful of that as I shared a very special birthday with my boy. The last three years with Jake's health had felt like a huge mountain. We had to grit teeth, battle on, lose our path and find it again; cajole and encourage each other even when tired beyond fatigue. We had to show the faith necessary to get to the summit. Research consistently tells us that even after reaching the summit the walker on the way down the mountain, is statistically more likely to injure themselves as they enter the valley.

There are usually only a few ways to get past the mountain. Going through it only applies in places like Mont Blanc on the motorway to Italy or in 'The Lord of the Rings' when the Fellowship travel through the Mines of Moria. Going around a mountain is hardly ever a realistic possibility and usually takes far too long. It usually takes us way off track and often results in far more stress and risk of injury for the walker. The only real option is to go over the mountain: but the walker knows it will cost them big style in energy, blood, (sometimes literally) sweat and tears.

So, as we climbed our final big mountain of the Camino, it felt appropriate to applaud the way Jake has climbed over his mountain. To climb and survive 2 Everest style 'Death Zone' moments, is miraculous. More than that though is the real class he showed in dealing with it. He is a strong character with a really strong faith and attitude to life. I'm proud of him.

I saluted Jake on his 19th birthday and encouraged him to seize his miracle and ensure his best was yet to come.

We passed the oldest tree on the Camino.

There was no journal entry from the Birthday Boy on Day 23. He was too busy partying!

TOTAL DISTANCE TRAVELLED: 664 km
DISTANCE TO SANTIAGO: 134 km

Chapter Twenty-Four

Sunday 23rd April 2017
Camino Day Twenty-Four:
O'Cebreiro to 10 km before Sarria

Day 24 was possibly our best day of the entire Camino.

A lack of Wi-Fi made it even more enjoyable. Sometimes it is good to down the electronic tools and gadgets of the modern world.

The Boston girls were out earlier than us the next morning, but we soon caught them up with Bart and Keith for a special sunrise photo where I snapped the girls jumping above the sun next to a huge stone sculpture of a Pilgrim. We walked and breakfasted together. The views were incredible, and we enjoyed more photos and views till about 11.00.

I get a bit of grief from my family and friends for always being a bit too optimistic. I suspect I am guilty as charged. Nicky often complains when I come out with a rose-coloured expression which usually starts with 'Well at least it didn't ...' that I'm unrealistic. I had reflected on that a fair bit whilst out on Camino and in the many conversations I had held with other pilgrims whilst out in Spain. My unscientific survey said that those pursuing the Camino experience are, in the main, optimists. I would venture to guess that a minimum of 95% of Peregrinos are optimists. I ask you, would a pessimist ever consider taking on a 500-mile challenge? I wondered…. and doubted it.

I don't say this to knock people who are by nature more pessimistic in their thinking. Remember my 'Everyone is different - Everyone matters' Calderdale Council post from a few days ago?

The Camino Pilgrim faces a fair few challenges along the way; it is a journey that entails some significant hardship. Of course, in modern times you can always decide to choose to go for that 5* hotel option. There is usually the either/or possibility in most of the larger sized villages across northern Spain. We had chosen the hostel route and have been all the richer for making that choice.

Most topics of Pilgrim conversation entail an early question about the state of each other's feet. I'd seen some seriously blistered feet. How some continued to walk day in day out I don't know. I was having to manage a pair of 8 day old 'mini' blisters. They were by no means terrible, but they still hurt. Two weeks ago, I tried to help a German guy for whom the Camino was clearly going to end early. He could barely walk and had taken 3-4 minutes to limp along a 20-metre corridor. I gave him a pack of some strong anti-inflammatory tablets plus a second set of drugs that prevented abdominal bleeding from the effects of the first. I was very careful to explain that the 2 needed to be used together. He understood I think, and I hope, he was either very trusting or in such significant pain that he didn't care. He took one of each there and then. Did he continue on the Camino? I don't know for sure, but I really think he would have had to pull out, he was in agony.

I really felt for him.

What was clear though, was that he wanted to carry on so much. His eyes showed a desperation to do so. I still like to hope that just maybe his optimistic nature (and some strong drugs) meant he could continue.

I've realised in the last few years, and particularly during Jake's illness, that I don't want to hang around pessimists for too long. I can get dragged down too easily and at 52 years of age I don't have any more time that. People boosters really are the best in my view. An upbeat and optimistic nature is so uplifting, and these are the people I want to hang around. I am thankful for 10-15 optimists who lift me in my work place every day. These optimists, in my view are the best of people to do life with.

The Camino has taught me that an optimistic comment can drag another 3-5 km out of a tired peregrino. That's why I had loved the company of Davinia, George, Keith, Bart, Molly, Kendra and many others on Camino. They didn't moan; they kept going and they kept encouraging me to keep going.

Dan and Harry were brilliant at this too. Just like Jake they never moaned once and that was so uplifting. Well done to the three amigos.

I chatted more deeply with Keith. I felt for him too. Like many ex-servicemen he carries a real burden from his time in the military and I felt quite privileged that he was so open with me. What we shared will remain private between us. He told me about the burden he had laid at the Cruz de Ferro. I truly hope it works out for him.

Our group then separated. Jake and I moved forward. They were in no rush, but we needed to push on if we were going to enjoy some downtime with Nicky and Rosie in Santiago before our return to the UK and return to normality. It felt sad and strange to leave the 4 of them behind, though we had all agreed to meet for a meal in Santiago on the following weekend.

I think Jake and I felt quite a sense of loss. We both walked quietly lost in our own thoughts. It was a similar sensation to when we had left Dan and Harry in Burgos. The bonds of friendship run much deeper on the Camino, I think.

Jake and I had decided that tonight we would 'wild camp' and so we proceeded to look for somewhere to sleep out. We found a perfect spot by a small stream in a field just 100 metres from the trail. Earlier we had spotted a clean 1-ton bag used for holding sand in the construction industry, so I walked back, rolled it up and brought it back to our chosen pitch and fashioned it with my penknife into a groundsheet. We packed it underneath with lots of fresh cut grass from the next field which we created a type of mattress under the sandbag.

We enjoyed a night to remember under the stars. This was 'the' experience of our whole Camino for both of us. Jake loved it. He was one happy peregrino.

We had a river bath, enjoyed a beer each and later made a fire. Perfection! As is ever the case when we Moorman boys mess around with designing wild fires, we had massively overestimated the amount of firewood we would need. We very graciously left a stack in that field, for the next intrepid pilgrim who wishes to camp out.

We stayed up with our fire until about 9.45 pm, but as it was getting progressively colder, we decided to get into our 'beds'.

Sleeping wasn't a problem. We were both shattered. Jake snuggled right down into his sleeping bag, only his nose and mouth was visible, protruding out of the baffle of his sleeping bag. Those sleeping bags were brilliant.

We need to give a big endorsement to Mountain Equipment, the sleeping bag manufacturers and especially to Geoff at BAC in Elland, UK who had provided them at a significantly discounted rate for our Camino. I slept in pyjama shorts and a tee shirt and was toasty warm, although my woolly hat needed to make an appearance just before dawn. Our sleeping bags were perfectly dry on the inside, though 'dewy damp' to touch on the outside.

Waking up to see the stars in their full glory was just magical. A full starry night, owls and a gently running stream that gave a musical accompaniment to Jake's snoring!

Day 24 of 27 was now walked and we had around 100 km left to walk to Santiago.

Yet again I was amazed by the bonds formed on Camino.

We had to split off from a group we'd been walking with for the past few days. Two of the American girls in this group (Molly & Kendra) I'd known less than 48 hours and yet they went out of their way to buy me a birthday card (signed by a multitude of nationalities) and a little gift. Just another example of how people here go above and beyond. Not having a dig but sometimes in life it's hard enough to get a 'happy birthday' text off people (I'm guilty of this too) but it filled me with positivity and hope when I realised yesterday that when all the complexities of life are stripped back, there are people who will go the extra mile to make your day.

Thank you Doc Keith, Bart, Kendra & Molly for making my birthday awesome and thank you to everyone back home who sent me love. I miss you all.

But the final and biggest thank you has to go to my dad who has given me the best ever experience. When yesterday I said I wanted to sleep under the stars he supported me again. Thank you, dad. You are the best.

Buen Camino

Ps sadly we have just 4 days left. We survived our camp out... just!

TOTAL DISTANCE TRAVELLED: 701 km
DISTANCE TO SANTIAGO: 97 km

Chapter Twenty-Five

Monday 24th April 2017
Camino Day Twenty-Five: Sarria to Portomarin

We got up at 07:05 and were packed and moving by 07:30. We had a big day ahead of us and we started well, with over 10 km of walking and breakfast completed by 09:15. When we facetimed home, we discovered Harry had broken his nose. Normal life in the Moorman household was obviously continuing.

It got very hot later in the morning and this slowed us down. Our old blisters resurrected themselves, as our feet swelled and protested at the heat and the effort. We were therefore, very relieved to roll into Portomarin at a later than estimated time of 3:30 pm. The prospect of our rejuvenation through showers and food was one we relished. Unbelievably, we knew that in just 3 days this adventure would end.

We had walked another 30+ km. The signposts and guide books for this section in Galicia were all a bit sketchy for Day 25. It left our total distance to Santiago somewhat uncertain, anything between 70 km and 92 km.

I first heard the saying 'the Camino provides' in the Martin Sheen film which we had watched as Jake was recovering from his first operation back in the Spring of 2014. I didn't pay much attention then, but when it started to become a strong possibility that we could actually take on this this trip in 2017, I started to hear the term more frequently used in online blogs and bulletins from the Confraternity of St James, the UK based Camino charity.

I remain a pragmatist at heart and I didn't really believe that the Camino provided at all. I did believe though that the Camino gives you the time, resources and space and the ability to focus on finding practical solutions to everyday Camino problems, especially as you have 'Camino Comrades' who will always seem willing to help you out with a problem. The spirit of togetherness that is so evident in the attitudes of so many Camino pilgrims, means that practical solutions can often be found for day by day difficulties.

Last night when we camped out under the stars, Jake and I shared our most special day on the Camino so far. The Camino really did provide.

In recent days we had continued our tradition of 'walking the Camino for ...' Today we 'walked for' people we knew who were sick with physical or mental health problems, for the brilliant medical team at Leeds General Infirmary who specialize in neurosurgery, especially Paul, Jake's surgeon, Dominic and Steve, the two anaesthetists who gave him such great operative care. It was Dominic who introduced me to 'Rule No 5 of the Velominati' midway through Jake's first surgery.

I still pinch myself as I ponder his bi-hourly contact throughout that operation on that very emotional and challenging day. Seriously how many families get an update call every 2 hours from the senior anaesthetist during a 7+ hour operation? He was amazing! We also walked for Christine, Paul's NHS secretary, who was so kind to us and never made us feel a nuisance with our all too frequent 'worried parent' phone calls and Lisa, a brilliant paediatric nurse on the Children's Ward at LGI, who gave Jake such fantastic nursing care.

Jake's Journal

Wow, words cannot do justice to just how cool last night was. I've camped loads of times, but this was way different. Basically, we only had sleeping bags, no tent, no mats so we had to improvise. Thankfully the Spanish weather allowed us to be fairly confident that we would be dry, and it worked out well for us.

We hadn't seen any snakes on the Camino until yesterday, where I saw two vipers both within a stone throw of our camping pitch. My nerves were a little edgy at times, but in the end those reptiles kept well away, so all was good.

In order to have some level of comfort, Dad and I found an empty rubble sack in a nearby barn and fashioned a make-shift ground sheet from it and stuffed it with grass. This produced a bed fit for a king (or so I first thought). We washed in the river which was a surprisingly pleasant temperature before lighting a fire and having some snacks and a drink.

When it came to sleep, about 5 minutes in, I realised we were on a slight slope and due to the many-layered sleeping arrangements it was fairly easy to slide down towards the river. Thankfully we both managed to avoid this, and the only other issue was that the outer part of the sleeping bags was a bit soggy from the dew. In the morning I also noticed that Dad's half of the bed had significantly more grass than mine which might explain why I woke up numerous times. Nevertheless, I'm actually even more grateful as my inability to sleep was rewarded with the sweetest canvas of stars I've ever seen. Honestly it was one the most beautiful things I've witnessed, so thank you Dad for your dodgy grass distribution.

We were both a little stiff this morning, yet we've managed to clear another 30+ km and are now not too far from Santiago and Mum and Rosie. Today's walk was pretty hot and tough, but I have to laugh; 700 km with nothing close to a real blister but now one has now finally got the better of me and my baby toe is a little sore. Thankfully a lovely Italian 'Chica' hooked me up with a plaster and we made it without further disaster to our albergue.

The past 24 hours have been awesome, I just want to keep walking ...

TOTAL DISTANCE TRAVELLED: 734 km
DISTANCE TO SANTIAGO: 64 km (approximately)

Chapter Twenty-Six

Tuesday 25th April 2017
'Camino Day Twenty-Six: Portomarin to Melide

The heat on Day 25 really did affect us, so we were relieved when today presented us with more typically British walking conditions. It was about 18 degrees, cool and damp; 'bread and butter' for 2 Yorkshire based pilgrims. My left heel blister continued to niggle me but despite a similar issue for Jake we both felt well, and we believed we could have walked 50 km if we had needed to.

By the end of the next day, we would only have around 20 km left to walk to meet the girls. So, there was no rush. The girls were flying out from the UK on 25th April to meet us!

We caught up with a number of familiar pilgrims, including Valerie from West Virginia. She looked fit and well and elated that she had walked so far. She was now hooked up with 2 Camino buddies, also from the States and she seemed really pleased and personally convicted that this experience had helped her. I really hoped that through this trip she has been able to lay down some of the burden of losing her daughter.

We also met up with Ivan from Hong Kong. He just seemed to turn up every now and then. He very much reminded me of a family friend Ian, from back home in Halifax. Different physiques maybe but very similar personalities. We also met up with Dave, a Cardiologist from Canada who we had spent an enjoyable evening with in the bell tower in Grañon. We also met Dave's 2 friends Jim and Jim: one from Ireland and the other from

Canada as well. They had walked a long way together and I strongly suspect they will be Camino buddies for years to come.

A few pilgrim walking styles were now very prominent. Lots of 'cowboy walking' was the norm. Jake and I had avoided it thankfully.

Day 26 was a tough one, for me at least. It made no sense really. It should have been a good day, but it felt even more tough than the Meseta road, now 11 days ago.

I saw a sign stuck in the wall which simply said: 'step by step.'

As the day unfolded and my sense of lethargy increased, I kept thinking about that sign and the simple truth it conveyed. In order to keep going I had to resort to just thinking of walking one step at a time.

I still don't understand why it felt so tough. On the previous night I'd probably had a better night's sleep under the stars than at any other time over the last 26 days. Feeling so lethargic made no sense to me. I should have been 'super stoked' to be so close to Santiago.

Isn't that a good analogy of life though? Far better sometimes to go 'step by step.'

So often we feel that we have something sorted and we then find an unforeseen circumstance occurs and we have to resort to a 'step by step' approach to try to recover all that lost momentum.

Last September was one of the hardest starts to a school year I have ever experienced in my teaching career of 30 plus years. The cumulative effect of failing drains, a leaky flat roof coupled with the school being massively overcrowded. The school was also project managing a £1.7 million fundraising campaign towards the total cost of a new £3.3 million Sixth Form and community centre in central Halifax. We also had 12 new staff and 32 year 7 students starting. Our previous highest student intake, in my 25 years at Ravenscliffe, had been 22! These factors all conspired to make it feel like a' 'Perfect Storm' and frankly I'd felt overwhelmed. As the school leader, I often feel I'm supposed to have the magic answer, utter something profound and make it all go swimmingly. Unfortunately, I felt pretty clueless at this time and there were many occasions when all I could say is 'I don't know!' My only solution was to advocate a 'step by step approach' At times I really did feel like Neville Chamberlain waving his piece of paper in the air and appeasing any number of people.

Given I resorted to step by step at school in September 2016, why was I so surprised that I needed go step by step yesterday? Life is often like that and I think we sometimes have to recognise that holding ground or taking just a little ground, is on occasions, good enough for a period of time. I realised at 1:30 pm on Day 26 that whilst we had about 12 km to go. we were still taking ground and by 4 pm I'd be through it. Sometimes we just have to grit our teeth and keep going 'step by step'.

We walked for Ravenscliffe yesterday. The whole community: its students, staff, parents and carers. Unbelievably I have worked there for 24 years. Why have I stayed? Because I love it! There is a great wider community connected to that school with so many people wanting to help to make good things happen there. Collectively we are moving forward step by step towards our Spring Hall Sixth Form Centre dream. I have no doubt it will come to pass, it is destined to happen.

(Footnote 2: Ravenscliffe@SpringHall opened to students on 1st September 2018.)

We finished Day 26 just 51 km from Santiago. What a day!

Jake's Journal

Today was bliss. It took a while to get into our rhythm, possibly as we set off without a specific target - knowing we just had to go as far as we could. Nevertheless, after pushing through the first 25 km before lunchtime we were both rewarded with a 'second wind'. I'd begun to forget what rain felt like so when it started to drizzle, I could have cried with happiness. The combination of hills, fields, forests now accompanied by grey skies instead of blue was ideal. I could have easily been back in Greetland, near Halifax: my home village. (Yes, I'm slightly homesick now).

Today I was definitely in my zone.

We arrived at our first potential albergue, and just blazed right past it. We passed more and more villages and ended up doing about 10 km more than we'd ever anticipated. We are now an easy 52 km away from Santiago with 2 days in which to do it so hopefully we can be a bit more chilled from here on.

Having said all of that, my feet are fairly sore right now, but the aches and pains are all part of the Camino.

Tonight, is our penultimate albergue night, and we managed to catch back up with Ivan, so we are set to have a great night.

It is scary to think a week today I'll be back to normal life but thankfully my thinking regarding the big return got totally renewed today. (I'll explain this later.)

TOTAL DISTANCE TRAVELLED: 776 km
DISTANCE TO SANTIAGO: 22 km

Footnote 1: I later heard from Dave, the Heart Surgeon from Canada, whilst I was walking the Camino de Finisterre in July 2018. He was just about to fly across

Canada to meet up once again with Canadian Jim. More evidence perhaps that the friendships made on Camino are likely to be longer term.

Footnote 2: Spring Hall Sixth Form Centre was opened on 27th September 2018 by Olympic and Paralympic athletes, Lord Sebastian Coe and Hannah Cockcroft.

Chapter Twenty-Seven

Wednesday 26th April 2017
Camino Day Twenty-Seven:
Melide to Pedrouzo (Arco do Pino)

The penultimate day's walking was fairly tough. We had walked a 42 and a 33 km walk on consecutive days and we were both very tired. Jake was in some pain from his hip, shin and that annoying blister between his little toes. Again, he never moaned once. He just kept walking.

I was often walking just behind him and found myself more and more mesmerised by the fact that I couldn't actually see the scar on his head from those 2 bouts of surgery. I was amazed and found myself craning my neck to scrutinise his scar without him realising. Yet again I was reminded that we really did get a miracle with that boy.

The afternoon's walking was quite laboured. We revived a little when we caught up yet again with the Hungarian Boys, minus Gabor who was some way back on the trail, plus Jay from America. We decided to cook tonight which usually would be no big deal but many of the hostels in Galicia have an unusual problem. They all have 5* showroom style kitchens, seriously good to look at but they possess not one single utensil. Not one spoon, one knife or one plate.

We wondered long and hard why this was so, the kitchen set up in each would easily cost £5,000 with cool touch hobs and trendy stainless-steel fridges. We rather darkly concluded that the hostels were in cahoots with the cafes and bars, no utensils meaning pilgrims would always have to pay to eat out!

We carefully chose the one hostel that did have a kitted-out kitchen. It was a lovely hostel costing the standard pilgrim fee of €10 each per night. Jay and Ivan decided to stay in and eat with us too, so I shopped and cooked for the four of us: chicken with garlic and a spicy sauce, vegetable chats, salad, bread and wine. It was lovely despite the fact that 6 other groups of pilgrims were also trying to cook on the only 3 available hobs. Later Max from Toulouse also turned up.

The hostel, rather bizarrely, had a sauna which we all decided to use, though 15 minutes of sweating was my limit. It was far too hot.

We all stayed up late on our last night and chatted. To be honest the hostel was pretty noisy anyway with a party of 60+ Spanish teenagers. They had started their Camino at Sarria, just 100 km from Santiago. This was obviously tactical as using Sarria as a starting point allows the pilgrim to claim a 'Compostela' in Santiago. Starting any nearer would mean no Pilgrimage Certificate. They really were a very loud group.

The atmosphere in the hostel in Pedrouzou (Arco do Pino) was hot! There was a real sense of anticipation as it was the last night of hostel living before reaching Santiago. We walked 33 km on Day 27 to leave us with just 21 km to go. I'm not certain that sleep was going to be easy on our last night. After all that walking it would be over in 24 hours. Such a weird sensation.

Our last night of albergue living was not a pleasure. Those Spanish teenagers were a nightmare. Having kept everyone awake beyond midnight, shouting, turning lights on and banging doors. There was no consideration shown for any other pilgrims. Their teachers were even worse. In trying to control their students, in which they were an abject failure, they made even more noise. If that was an indication of the Spanish education system, which I'm sure it isn't, then thank goodness for the English system (even with all its flaws.)

Tomorrow we would meet up with Nicky and Rosie.

Football had to come into it at some point, obviously!

Sadly, as a Bristol City FC fan I'm very well acquainted with abject failure. As ever, it is the hope that kills me! In my 40+ years of supporting that team, I've had multiple disappointments and very few 'seasons to be cheerful.' But football is in my blood and I continue to dare to dream.

Amazingly my 2 Yorkshire born sons are mad keen Bristol City fans too. There are no glory seeking 'plastic' fans in our house. The girls unfortunately have yet to see the light, but we live in hope for them.

Tonight, I saw a friends Instagram post about Liverpool FC, highlighting the famous Kop singing 'You'll never walk alone!' Their post must have referred to a Liverpool game from sometime during this last week, I'm guessing it does anyway? I've been a bit distracted recently and lost track of football this I month, apart from the Bristol City scores of course!

When the Liverpool Kop are in full voice, especially on a European Champions League night, under the floodlights, the mass rendition of that song is seriously spine tingling. I was at their Anfield stadium, when Bristol City famously dumped them out of the FA cup in 1994 and the Kop were immense in their graciousness at that defeat. They were still noisy, until 9,000 Bristol City supporters countered with 'Drink up thee Cider'. It was a super special night for our fans. Sadly, one of the very few!

The Camino, for many Peregrinos, is a journey they make alone. But many of these individual travellers will confirm to you that they actually travel together within the Camino Family. Juan, the oft mentioned Spaniard on his 28th journey back to France confirmed this when he told me that the Camino was and is his only family.

You and I may argue of course that his is an escapist route too far. There was definitely an element of nobility in his never ending journey. Essentially a homeless pilgrim, Juan 'worked his ticket' by volunteering to help at a hostel every night, in return for board and lodgings.

The fact is that almost every traveller I have spoken to on this Camino, has confirmed that conversations with their fellow pilgrims is a highlight of the experience. I am certain that I will be seeing some of my fellow pilgrims again, but only this time in their home cities like Eindhoven, Boston, Pisa, British Columbia, Budapest, Barcelona and Galway. The bond has been established. None of us 'ever walked alone!'

So, it is with life. Some of us will hold onto a faith, others will put their trust in human relationships, and many will do both. Whatever! If we choose to invest and nurture our effort into relationships, we really will 'never walk alone!'

Relating back to Jake's illness. As a family we experienced outrageous acts of kindness like the Robinson family turning up at the hospital in Leeds on a freezing Saturday morning in 2016 with hot bacon sandwiches for Nicky and myself. Their kindness was nuts! Or Jill, one of my school Governors leaving a Shepherd's Pie on the door step. Jill is a practising doctor and a massively busy lady. Nuts again! Or Howard and Brenda, Chris and Donna or Helen and Garry, neighbours of ours, feeding us with a meal as one or both of us rolled back home at 11 pm or later from LGI for a night of 'rest' after a gruelling day at the hospital. Or Nicky's Mum who drove to Leeds every day to sit with Jake and give Nicky a breather. All examples of unbelievable kindness over a long period of time!

We never walked alone, just like all the Camino Pilgrims before us, who have walked this route over the last thousand years. History tells us they too received unconditional love and kindness along the Way.

The Moorman family never walked alone during the years of 2014-2016. I really appreciated that then and I appreciated it even more now.

My point?

If we want to avoid walking alone, we must never stop trying to invest in relationships.

I believe that just 2 things ultimately define the success of my school, indeed any organisation: the quality of relationships and the quality of communication. The best staff at my school do both really well daily.

If Jake and I want the 'Camino Spirit' to shine in our lives, we need to try to ensure 'we never walk alone.'

We walked the Camino today, for all the people who have supported us so massively with this 'little challenge.' Over 260 'Justgiving' online sponsors and over 100 cash donors, amongst them was the staff communities at Doc Martens footwear in Camden, London, where Rosie worked her internship year in 2016 who donated £493. There was also the staff community at Leo Group, Halifax, who sponsored us £500 and the school community at Skyswood Primary School in St Albans, Hertfordshire, where Bob, my college friend from 32 years ago, is Headteacher. They raised us £500. I hadn't even seen Bob throughout those 32 years. It was all nuts. We hadn't even met most of these people and probably never would, but I guessed they have been touched by Jake's story and of course Brain Tumour Research is a great cause.

We have never felt that we walked alone.

Jake's Journal

Today was our penultimate day of walking and for me it was definitely a 'grit your teeth' kind of day.

We have now walked 112 km in the last 3 days alone making these past few days our biggest physical push by far. For this reason, each hour today was hard, I didn't necessarily ever feel like I was in my zone unlike yesterday and at one point I just had to stop and sit down for a bit. However, regardless of all this we completed 33 km in under about 6 hours of walking time.

All along the Camino we have been known as the 'tall English boys who walk fast' and today I maybe took this a bit far - a local young man overtook us in one of the towns today (probably just in a rush to work) but having not been overtaken for 26 days I got a little competitive. I then proceeded to click up a gear and overtake the man, I don't think he even noticed, and my only reward was an increase in aches and pains for the remaining 4 hours.

I was super glad to arrive at our albergue today and from where I sit it is only 21 km to Santiago de Compostela and the end of our journey. We met up with our three Hungarian friends again, as well as the famous Ivan (the selfie king of the Camino) and Jay. I think our last night in an albergue is going to be a good one!

Today we also met a pair of nuns from Mexico. This was super cool and the attitude that they gave off in just a 10-minute conversation was amazing. Once they heard my story, Sister Veronica said; 'We have definitely found what we were looking for on this Camino'.

I then thought about all of our Camino friends who have already arrived in Santiago and those who will arrive after us, I really hope they will all find what they're looking for. As dad said before: 'The Camino Provides'.

Buen Camino.

Why the discrepancy in the distances walked?

Clearly, we didn't have minus 21 km left to walk. We had 21 km left. I've wondered that all the way though the writing of this book.

The official 'Compostela' we claimed in Santiago stated that we walked 799 km from St Jean Pied de Port to Santiago. But our official distanced combined, as measured via our guidebook and the Camino Frances App, took us to a total of 828 km.

There are potentially 2 contributing reasons:

Firstly; the Spanish wayside signs in Galicia simply did not add up. Within minutes of passing one sign, we would pass another which stated up to 10 km more or less. Secondly, we had also walked some significant extra distances when we chose the 'alternativo' routes including the 'Camino Dura' (Harder Way) and that most pointless of bridges in Astorga.

Whichever and whatever! We knew we had easily walked in excess of 800 km or 500 miles.

TOTAL DISTANCE TRAVELLED: 807 m
DISTANCE TO SANTIAGO: -21 km

Chapter Twenty-Eight

Thursday 27ᵗʰ April 2017
Camino Day Twenty-Eight:
Pedrouzo (Arco do Pino) to Santiago de
Compostella

The noise of the Spanish teenagers meant that by 5 am many of the pilgrims in our room of 30 beds had given up on sleep and adopted the 'if you can't beat them, join them attitude.' Instead, I chose to write up my last Camino journal and was so caught up in it that I failed to see Jay, Ivan and The Hungarian Boys get up and leave. I only noticed their absence when I got up for a shower at 6:45 am Jake and I were on our way by 7:30 am.

Despite us being very relaxed with our walking speed on this our last day, we still seemed to gobble up the kilometres. I suspect I was correct about the inaccuracy of those Spanish signs after all. This meant we were able to stop for a coffee at 10 am and still be confident enough to tell the girls that we would be in the main square in front of Santiago Cathedral by noon.

At 12.01 we duly arrived in the main plaza and Jake, pine cone in his hand, ran the last 100 meters to launch himself at his Mum, as a lone piper piped us through the archway into the square.

What an awesome moment. One we will never forget.

We had literally walked 500 miles to see these 2 girls. They looked wonderful, identically dressed in denim and dark glasses, clearly 'peas from the same biological pod'.

I realised yet again, at that moment, just how much I loved my girls. It was very emotional. Of course, we would have loved Harry to have been there with us too. Whilst he couldn't we were very grateful that we had enjoyed 12 days of this special experience with him.

We walked the 5 minutes from the Cathedral to the Airbnb, where we enjoyed a warming coffee and a leisurely catch up. Santiago was freezing cold on our last day, clearly preparing us for the return to England and its wonderful weather. The girls would simply not believe that we had enjoyed 24 days of continual warm sunshine, until they had left England! Unfortunately for them they had turned up with shorts and T-shirts with the temperatures nearer to 10 than 20 degrees and a biting north easterly wind.

We pottered around Santiago. It felt weird having no rucksack to carry. We witnessed Jay finish his Camino and enjoyed a beer with Bryson, our Aussie friend, who was the very first pilgrim we had met when we entered the hostel in St Jean Pied de Port with my sister Liz, 28 days and a whole lifetime ago.

The Hungarian Boys and Ivan finished with Dave the Heart Surgeon, Jim and Jim, plus Kate from Liverpool who we had met briefly back at O'Cebreiro on the day before Jake's 19th birthday. Everyone was tired but happy. All were quite emotional.

We had finished! 799 OFFICIAL KILOMETRES, (plus quite a few extras) were walked in 28 days. We were now in Santiago and had the thrill of Nicky and Rosie being there to meet us!

WOW: words cannot describe the feelings!

I must admit that throughout our Camino I had kept it half in mind for us to do that latter Finisterre route (95 km or so extra) as an add on. During the last 2 weeks we had pushed on well and we could have actually positioned ourselves with enough time to do it. However, I never raised the possibility with him. In my view that would not have been in the spirit of this Camino and we would then have lost 3 of the 4 days we had with the girls in Santiago. It could wait, we did what we came here to do, loved every minute of it, but we love the girls even more. They are super precious to us.

Cape Finisterre was going no place soon. It would still be there and in the words of Arnie Schwarzenegger (hopefully) 'I'll be back!'

I hoped Nicky would return with me to do this 'lightweight' walk sometime in the future. I think she might well enjoy the peregrino experience as I had.

I also knew that I was a quite tired and needed to recover before butting out of the 'Camino Bubble' of the last month and returning to family, life and work in Yorkshire on 2nd May. It would be back to work for me in 4 days' time and at 52 years old I realised as Rosie, Harry and Jake delighted in reminding me all too frequently I needed to pace myself these days. A few days off in Santiago therefore seemed wise and justified.

On one of our last Camino days Jake and I had walked closely side by side using one earphone each to listen to the George Ezra song 'Blind man in Amsterdam'

The lyrics 'When this adventure ends the next one will begin' really struck a chord with me, definitely the right words for the day we actually rolled into Santiago.

This had been THE complete adventure.

From the minute my little sister Lizzie welcomed us into Biarritz airport with my nephew Dan 28 days ago, we have lived and breathed the Camino, firstly as a 'Gang of Four' with Harry and Dan, then a 'Dynamic Duo', just Jake and me.

It has been one of the best experiences of my life: completely cathartic as we finally closed the 2-year period of illness that Jake battled so well. It has also been something that has made me feel totally optimistic about the future, his, mine, my family's and my schools, particularly as we prepared to move onto the next 'Camino type' stages of our lives.

This Camino experience would end on Monday 1st May 2017 when we fly back to the UK (Three years to the day since Jake's first surgery.) Our 'Camino of Life' in Halifax, West Yorkshire will continue, and I am now recharged and 'up for' the challenges that will come with this new 'Way'.

What I have really discovered in these last 28 days is that you don't need to actually do something super innovative or whacky like the Camino to find your 'Own Way', you just have to try and do life well. Better day by day, every day. That means intentionally spending more time seeking to become more compassionate, trying harder to be better in what you do, making more of a difference for people, seizing the day more, being more generous, more thankful, relishing more time with people and understanding better that people really do matter.

I am content to emphasise that this journey has had a big spiritual element for us as a family. Simply put we came to say, 'Thank You'.

Be under no illusion, I don't exaggerate this point. I remember lying awake all night in the early hours of the mornings of 1st May 2014 and 9th February 2016 fearing that I was going to lose my son. When the 'D' word is mentioned on 2 separate occasions to a young lad aged 16 and then 17, then the odds go completely askew. You brick it! I bricked it! That night Psalm 91 sustained me, it is worth a read, particularly if you find yourself in a dark moment.

I prayed like I never prayed before and I was so fortunate that I had other people praying with me those 2 nights.

Nicky, Tony, Sarah, Steve, my Mum, Nicky's mum Jenny and many more.

On the morning of his second operation in February 2016 it seemed that Jake would have to face it being postponed as they needed a special separate room on the High Dependency Ward for his care post-surgery. At 11:00 am there was still no bed available. The nurses told us to prepare to go home. Within 15 mad minutes that all miraculously changed. Messages were shared in that quarter of an hour and following the prayers of many people a bed was suddenly released and the rest as they say is history.

I'm totally aware that some of you will not believe this faith part of our story. I'm telling it you as it is and trying to be emotionally neutral. This account is as factual as I can be. You may feel it was all a big coincidence, but it was my conviction then and remains so now that it was God influenced.

I know some may sit and read this post and scoff about modern day miracles and flukes. How long ago did Alastair Campbell infamously say 'We don't do God? That of course is your right, but I know that the prayers of those faithful people engineered a miraculous reversal of fortune for Jake. All of those prayers were answered.

Why was Jake spared and others in similar life-threatening situations aren't? I have no idea and would not presume to patronise you with glib and trite answers.

What I know unshakeably is that our prayers were heard, and we saw Jake pull through thanks to the wonderful skills of Paul and his team in Leeds.

And so, that is why today I found a quiet corner in the cathedral in Santiago and uttered my own quiet prayers of complete gratitude and thanksgiving.

When I was asked to present my 'Credential' in Santiago containing over 80 confirmatory ink stamps of our appearance in hostels, restaurants and public buildings across this 500-mile trek across northern Spain during the last 28 days, I was completely honest answering the accreditation officer's question in an exchange that was worded something like this:

"Why did you choose to walk the Way of St James?"

"For spiritual reasons, to say thank you to God for sparing my son and to say thank you in a practical way to the incredible medical staff based in Leeds who have been blessed with such a wonderful skill."

I cannot give you a more straight or honest answer.

Jake's survival, not once but twice, was miraculous and I am convinced God has a purpose for his life.

I'm sure he will have a part to play at some time in the future, in supporting other people as they try to deal with the traumatic effects of brain haemorrhage.

So, our journey concluded but continues. I'm now just a whole heap wiser and more prepared to try to do life better, to go on and attempt to make my own impact better, in its own small way, in 2017 and beyond.

Jake's Journal

28 days
800 km
210 hours of walking
1000 x "Buen Caminos"
1,036,319 steps
2 countries
and 1 birthday later

WE HAVE ARRIVED.

It's insane to think that everything over the last month has been about reaching that far off place called Santiago de Compostela, and yet here we are. I cannot believe that what started as just a 'cool idea' has actually ended up happening.

The Camino has exceeded all expectations, we aimed for 30 days and did it in 28, we aimed to raise £5,000 and have currently raised over £12,000. But apart from the numeric evidence that this trip was special, I know completely and utterly that the last month has been the greatest experience of my life.

There were times when I felt crap and had to just get on with it. There were times when it felt like the easiest thing in the world, but since that first day in the Pyrenees I knew this was going to be epic.

I have learnt so much, I can now introduce myself in Cantonese but more importantly I have learnt that one backpack and a good attitude is more than enough to live the greatest life ever.

We have mentioned a few phrases that are often uttered by pilgrims on the Camino such as 'the Camino provides'. I am now going to introduce you to another saying- 'El Camino no termina en Santiago' -'the Camino does not end in Santiago'. Of course, the physical aspect ends here but I've come to realise that the Camino is not and never was just a walk, it is the best analogy for life I can think of and it is because of this that the Camino will continue for me well after I have left Spain.

During the last week as I became aware that this day was approaching, I could not help but be saddened at the thought of returning to 'normal' life. But now understanding this concept I have realised that the real challenge here is not to walk 500 miles. The real challenge is to take the spirit of the Camino back home with me and to live the best life I can.

I came on the Camino to say thank you and I'm leaving even more thankful than when I arrived. The fact is I nearly died twice. I could have been permanently brain damaged, paralysed or mute. But I am 100% healthy and living life to the full.

Thank you to everyone who has encouraged and supported us and everyone who has made this possible, especially my family! I'm incredibly proud of Dad and me and of course Harry and Dan.

I'll be returning home with mixed emotions but a huge thankfulness that the adventure continues back in England.

I'm 19 (just) and have been so blessed to experience all that I have at such a young age, from brain surgery to blisters, I would not change a thing!

P.S. Regarding the pine cone that Dad mentioned, I found it whilst walking the 'Camino Dura' about a week ago. Mum loves pine cones so I decided I'd take it for her, pretty simple really. So, as I hugged Mum, I gave her the pine cone that I'd carried 180 km for her. She likes it!

Buen Camino

TOTAL DISTANCE TRAVELLED: 828 km
DISTANCE TO SANTIAGO: 0 km!

Chapter Twenty Nine

Post Camino Day 1
Santiago de Compostella

Boy! The little things in life have suddenly become a joy! And I appreciate them all. Creature comforts are back on the menu. There is much to appreciate.

We appreciate the fact that we now have 2 loos to use without the concern that there might be desperate pilgrims queueing up fourfold outside (It is good to be rid of that psychological pressure.) I love the fact that this accommodation is not paperless!

I made a coffee quickly followed by a second. Luxury.

I had a lie in, nearly 2 hours extra in bed. My first in over a month and I was now back with my wife too.

I slept in a comfortable bed with sheets.

I had no snoring companions from the 'League of Nations' with their faces less than 1 metre from mine.

I didn't have to use a damp smelling towel. Those in the Airbnb were freshly laundered and smelt of soap-powder not sweat.

So many reasons to be cheerful!

It felt weird not to be walking! We should be walking. By now 7:45 am we should have walked 3-5 km at least.

We collected our Compostela's yesterday evening before a celebratory meal with the girls. Collecting it was very special. Jake was genuine when he said this certificate was more precious to him than his A levels (Michael Gove, former UK Education Secretary please note.)

I knew what he meant.

We are both going to frame them and our Credentials with their 80 odd, personalised stamps linking us to a moment in time where we stayed or visited a hostel, cafe or church. Every time I got a new stamp on 'The Way' I got a childlike thrill, just like I did as a kid when I collected my next animal bone, skull, stamp or beer mat!

Nicky suggested my framed certificates and Credential should go in the downstairs toilet. No way! They are going in prime position in my office at school!

My three big fears pre-Camino failed to fully materialise. I refer to the 3 dreaded B's.

BLISTERS: we did have them, but all 4 of us managed them well. I remember early doors Dan and I both had a Mohican style blister on our little toes, the skin had folded over to create a punk style extension. We never really suffered like so many others. You may remember Jem, 'The Hobbling Pilgrim from Astorga?' That was not our Camino experience. Phew!

BEDBUGS: we never saw them, and we never heard of them thankfully. It may well be that they are the stuff of

Camino Legend, a bit similar to the way the British love to exaggerate snow. Person 1 says, it's going to snow, Person 2 says, it will be a couple of inches and Person 3 informs us, that it will be a blizzard with all the schools out: all communication done and dusted in a 3-minute time period.

Even now just the mention of the 'Bedbug' word makes me itch!

BRAIN SURGERY: Thankfully there is nothing further to report!

The Camino has confirmed to me that life can still be enjoyed even if your lifestyle is chaotic, but a bit of preparation can make it so much better. In my school context, I believe that some of the very best staff have a common thread in being organised, and because they are organised, they are so much more efficient with time, energy and resources and so achieve much better results.

My encouragement to anyone reading this who can't honestly claim to be good in that area is to improve. Even those who prepare well can get better. Target some self-development in your preparations for daily life and in my view your enjoyment of life will become a whole lot better and more rewarding.

So, in Santiago I resolved to try to improve myself.

As the house continued to sleep, I decided to re-enter my Ravenscliffe world even though it was not a pay day for me as it was my last of 13 unpaid days of leave of absence.

The iPad that Nicky brought out to Spain with her, contained 394 school email messages. I was thinking strategically and reckoned I could deal with 2 types of disposal simultaneously if I started to deal with them whilst sat on the toilet! How many emails could I lose before the sleeping beauties and his lordship upstairs started to rise?

On a more serious note, I decided I will walk later this morning, just myself for an hour or so to Santiago Cathedral, and into the chapel of St James to give my thanks.

I will walk for: Katherine, Angela, Bill and Hazel, Amanda and Tony, 6 members of our Ravenscliffe community. They have all lost loved ones in recent times, for some, very recent times; one of them has the ordeal of a funeral today. I wished I could be there to support them, even though I'm 1200+ miles away I can still root for them and so I wanted to 'walk for them.'

Chapter Thirty

Post Camino Day 2
Santiago de Compostella

Cool Down

Our first day in Santiago felt strange.

It felt like we should be walking and yet apart from walking parts of the old city of Santiago, which is relatively compact, we did very little.

My iPhone steps indicator showed just 10,000 steps compared to a daily average of 37,000 steps over the preceding 28 days.

Apparently today I had managed 8 steps though this proved that the technology can't actually be that accurate as I was sleeping two floors up and that's 30 steps minimum!

We really enjoyed tootling around Santiago with no pressure to do anything too exerting. We did tourist stuff like having a coffee in the Cathedral plaza, chatting to folk we had got to know in the preceding 29 days, meeting pilgrims as they completed their Camino, eating ice cream and such like.

Nicky even squeezed in an hour's sunbathe with her book. It was warm in the afternoon on today, but rain and 12 degrees maximum temperatures were forecast for tomorrow, our last full day in Santiago. I ruefully saw this as an unwelcome preparation and reality check for flying back to the UK and its bespoke weather systems.

We really enjoyed the chance to meet back up with two pilgrims who we had met and grown to really like on Camino. Valerie was the American lady from Virginia we had chatted to way back on the walk towards Astorga. In just 2 short verbal exchanges of less than 30 minutes each Valerie and I had really connected at a deep level. Our short chat impacted on me massively. She had lost her 24-year old daughter and was walking the Camino in her memory. Yet another example of someone having a reason for walking the Camino.

She was eating lunch with a couple of Americans in a square near the cathedral. I guess they will now stay in touch for life. That is what the Camino does for you, that shared and intense experience makes friends for life. Valerie was lovely. I really hoped this experience has helped her a little in trying to come to some sort of terms with her loss. It was another tangible reminder for the Moorman family of just how blessed we were with Jake's outcomes. It could have been so different.

We also enjoyed meeting back up with Bryson from Australia. The girls loved him and were in awe of his ability to lipread so well. We swapped some more football related banter, as I have said previously, some aspects of life always seem to come back to football.

He was a character back in St Jean at the outset of our Camino and an even bigger character now we had got to know him better. I massively respected his outlook on life. Profound deafness must present so many social barriers to day to day living and yet I doubt anything would hold Bryson back. He clearly gets on with life day by day and embraces all of its challenges. He sneaked me in through a back passageway of the Cathedral into the sepulchre of St James, meaning we both avoided a massive queue. Naughty I know, but I was a totally innocent party to this deed! Apparently, the finger of St James is kept as a religious artefact in this sepulchre, though all I could see was a bright silver box. There was plenty of reverence in that crypt though it didn't do much for me to be honest, but another mighty lesson of the Camino sprang to mind as I watched other pilgrims venerate that chapel - each to their own.

Nicky and Rosie were brilliantly gracious when meeting all these people, it must have felt like they were attending the work Christmas Party of their partner. We have all had that overwhelming experience when you get introduced to masses of unknown people, whose names you instantly forget. A "Get me out of here!" reaction would be totally understandable. Fair play to the girls, they had been brilliantly gracious since we arrived in Santiago.

Just as the weather has started to cool down, so had the intensity of this Camino experience, it has to, I guess. Once you stop walking the intensity wanes.

I think for Jake and I there would necessarily be a period of readjustment. Whilst ecstatic to have finished and to be with the girls, both of us were definitely missing the Camino. This seemed a crazy feeling, until I started to ponder a bit deeper. Research shows that top athletes and footballers recover quicker when they follow a cool down routine. I guessed that Jake and I were doing something similar though the analogy with top athletes ends right there. We were just cooling down.

People have said many nice things to us in the last month and we had been very appreciative of their messages. The truth is though that we were not top athletes, we were and are nothing special. We are, and I hope will remain, relatively 'normal' English boys, blessed with a longer than average stride. We got into a good rhythm on this journey, early on. helped massively by two great pacesetters in Harry and Dan. The truth is that anyone can walk the Camino. We were pretty quick in 28 days, but there were many who were quicker. We saw pilgrims of all shapes and sizes: Plodders, Trudgers, Shufflers, Beefy Berts, 70-80-year olds, Red Facers, Sweaty Betties, Returnees, First Timers, Dig Deepers and Cyclists with no bells.

Cooling down for us means getting back into the swing of daily living. At home Nicky has a list of jobs waiting. Our cellar conversion needs some serious builder attention and school will no doubt challenge me again. The costs of our Spring Hall new build have risen another £80,000 whilst we were away and we were, like many schools projected to possibly go into budget deficit in 12 to 24 months once we start to be accountable for costs of running a second premises.

Life will not be easy, the cool down had begun.

Chapter Thirty One

Post Camino Day 3
Santiago de Compostella

For a final Santiago-based link it really had to come down to a final quote from my favourite book and our number one family film: The Lord of the Rings.

When the boys were little and we went out for a walk or we played on beaches, mountains or in the woods, we always ended up playing 'Lord of The Rings.' As the Dad, I always had first pick of the characters and so would consistently choose to be Aragorn, the true hero of that epic story in my view. Jake and Harry were never happy about that as they too wanted to be Aragorn. I always won the wooden sword fights, a 38-year old Dad, against a 6-year old and a 4-year old was always going to be the favourite in jousting terms; even when they combined forces and attacked with stealth from front and rear! Jake would often enlist the help of his school friend Matthew, both of them dressed in full knight's regalia, but I was still the overcomer. They certainly became a more effective fighting 'Urukai' in the latter part of their teenage years.

> "All that is gold does not glitter,
> Not all those who wander are lost;
> The old that is strong does not wither,
> Deep roots are not reached by the frost.
> From the ashes a fire shall be woken,
> A light from the shadows shall spring;
> Renewed shall be blade that was broken,
> The crownless again shall be king.

'The Lord of the Rings' by JRR Tolkien.

On Monday 1 May 2017, we closed our own epic adventure with a final thank you to the many Peregrinos who had helped us to achieve what we never thought before 2016 to be possible.

Thank you to: Hannah (the Meseta Queen) and her fellow Germans, Thomas, who beat Jake at chess playing blindfolded and Stefan who wielded the most ferocious pocket knife imaginable, Bryson, Patrick and Clayton from Australia who proved to be great fun, Thomas from Austria, the man with the biggest smile on Camino, Davide from Italy, definitely the coolest of policemen and also Erica from Italy the only pilgrim to have beautifully manicured and painted nails for the whole trip, 'Mad'

Max, who with Daniel my nephew, proved to be super crazy Frenchmen, Marek from Poland who most days walked 50 km on 2 false knees, Davinia and Manalo from Spain, super fun amigos despite the language barrier (for me at least), Frank and Cesar from Spain who were the most sensitive of pilgrims and never made a sound when we shared a room with them. They couldn't speak English and I couldn't speak Spanish, but we understood and liked each other. There was Maria from the Czech Republic who was as crazy as Marek, Valerie, Bill, Cathy, Denis and Jay, who proved that our American cousins are a truly classy crew and also David and Libby (Kendra's uncle and mum) who were great company right at the end of our Camino. George from Canada remains the best ranger I have ever met, 'Ivan the Terrible', from Hong Kong, who was the king of selfies and who just kept appearing along the trail from nowhere, the crazy Philippine gang who caught taxi after taxi and treated us to lovely chocolate ice cream in León, Kate from Liverpool and Suzanne and Erica from England who sponsored us so kindly in Estella and cried at Jake's story, Antonio from Brazil, Hersht from Iceland and Seoin from Korea, who kept calling me 'Captain Martin', Colb from Denmark, Jim and Dave from Canada, a retired accountant and still practising heart surgeon, Jim from Ireland, the three Hungarian Boys, Joel, Gabor and George who ate onion and chorizo goulash morning noon and night, and the final formidable foursome of Bart from Holland, Keith from Ireland and Molly and Kendra from the USA who we hope we will see again.

They were all the best of company. Thank you to all of the pilgrims we met, named and unnamed. We won't forget you; especially the two 'non-singing nuns!'

Finally, my personal thanks goes to Harry, Jake and Daniel for making this such a special family event and the ultimate 'Dad and Lads' experience.

The final image we took away from Santiago with us is from the Pilgrims mass on Saturday when we got to see the botafumeiro (incense burner) swung by 7 strong and cassocked men. It was a super special moment.

Our massive thanks go one final time, to the many people who supported our BTRS cause so brilliantly. We aimed for £5,000. Through the amazing generosity of so many, and an amazing £1000+ donation in June 2017

from Wilkinson Woodward Solicitors, Halifax we finally raised over £15,000.

Footnote:
18 months later in December 2018 I read in the national press that 2 altar boys had been sacked by the cathedral authorities in Santiago for secretly dumping half a pound of weed in the botafumeiro incense burner.

Apparently witnesses in attendance, reported that it was thought to be one of the most relaxed services in the last millennium!

Chapter Thirty Two

June 2017

2017 had already been an epic year for our family: but there was still plenty to come.

The best of news in June 2017

Harry has a paid internship starting in Cambridge this month. Rosie is exploring post university options having already been assured of gaining a top degree. Her wedding looms in just over a year. Nicky continues to look amazing and to be the rock of this family. I pinch myself daily to think I actually got the girl! The 'Boy Wonder' himself, Jake is due to start at University of Leeds in September and has the brightest of futures in front of him.

Jake has just received the best news we could have ever asked for. He has been given the all clear and a discharge notice.

Paul, his neurosurgeon, said: "I'll see you in a year's time, but that is purely precautionary."

Jake grabbed a mandatory selfie with the man who will always be a true hero to our family.

Jake's Journal

Saturday 14 October 2017 was significant. As many of you know nearly 18 months-ago I underwent lifesaving neurosurgery for the second time in an attempt to cure a brain disorder that had adversely affected every aspect of my life for the previous two years. After the initial ten hour surgery, I thankfully awoke and began the long journey to full recovery.

Whilst on this journey I became aware of just how fortunate I had been to survive what so many sadly do not. When you get told that there is a strong chance that you're going to die tomorrow, your entire perspective shifts. When you realise you didn't die, it shifts even more. I began to sense a unique sense of responsibility to do something not only to help others who were enduring similar circumstances to me but also simply to say thank you to the people who are the reason I am alive today.

In the following weeks, a perfect opportunity began to emerge. Whilst still confined to a wheelchair, my dad and I watched a film titled 'The Way' it was about a historic pilgrimage route from the South of France to Santiago de Compostela in North-West Spain. This route is known as The Camino De Santiago.

The film had barely finished when dad and I gave each other 'the look', we knew what we had to do.

Preparation began for our big adventure, our chosen charity was Brain Tumour Research & Support, (BTRS) based in Leeds. This charity offers essential help to individuals suffering from brain trauma as well as their families and also carries out vital research into the causes of brain-related trauma.

Our plan was in place and we set a fundraising target of £5000, something we thought was achievable given the scale of our challenge, but also a target that was realistic. However, we were painfully aware that this barely covered even a fraction of the cost of my treatment. Nevertheless, 'every little helps', so we launched our fundraising campaign.

On Friday 27th April, 28 days and 500 miles since our very first steps on the Camino, Dad and I walked into Santiago de Compostela. On Saturday 14th October, over three years since I received my first diagnosis, a year since we started campaigning, we handed over £15,184 to BTRS. This money is to save lives. This money is to say thank you for saving mine.

If there is anything that I've learnt from my own story, it is the following. However rubbish your situation might feel in the moment, you always have an opportunity and a choice in how you respond to it. There can be good even in the worst of circumstances.

Have a great day and 'Buen Camino.'

Jake x

In typical Jake style, he celebrated his news, dressed up as Gandalf at a fancy-dress party, in a costume made by his mum.

Part Three

An early and unexpected return

November 2017 to August 2018

The Camino de Finisterre and Muxia circuit

I never for one moment expected to be back walking a Camino in Santiago, less than 15 months after we finished the previous one. But this was the reality in July 2018.

The intervening months since flying home in May 2017 have been good. Everything seemed to be on a roll. Jake his brother and sister were healthy, and Jake had been discharged.

Nicky and I were very happy.

On 29th November 2017, my whole world turned upside down as I was hit with the devastating and totally unexpected news that my sister Anna, aged 57, had died. Her death was tragic and totally unforeseen.

I had never suffered a close family bereavement and I felt for the first time in my life, the numbing and nauseating effects of total grief. We are a close family, it devastated us all. We loved Anna and we miss her.

Christmas 2017 and New Year 2018 came and went in a blur. I know that I was of no use to my family at that time. The tragic loss of my sister Anna, in late November 2017 was devastating.

Anna was my middle sister; she was the 'glue that stuck' our family together. She loved us all and would regularly check in to see how things were going, especially in the tougher times. She cared and subscribed to the view that 'actions speak louder than words.'

As a senior nurse at St Mary's Hospice in Birmingham on the night shift for 21 years, Anna had supported hundreds of people in their final hours with dignity, compassion and care. She made those final hours more bearable for people afflicted with life ending conditions.

I grew to understand in the intervening six months, that I am the sort of person who needs to do something positive to help me manage my grief. It was in late January 2018, that I began to think that maybe a better way of dealing with this grief would be to go back to Santiago and to walk another Camino. I remembered the saying, 'Every Pilgrim has a reason' and I certainly had my reason.

I commitment to the double challenge of walking a 100 km Camino in northern Spain, with five other members of my family and then running the Birmingham half marathon in autumn 2018 with 6 other members of Anna's extended family.

I had no doubt that I would love the Camino. The Birmingham half marathon however filed me with a little more fear. I suffered with early osteoarthritis in my knees, so I knew this one could hurt. However, my sister's memory deserved to be celebrated and the opportunity to do so through both these events would make any pain I felt in doing them, a bit more bearable.

Our actions as a family within these challenges might actually speak far louder and with far more eloquence, than any words we could say in tribute to a sister we all loved dearly.

From that seed of an idea, fast forward another 6 months and I was back on the Pilgrim Trail to walk the 'The Camino de Finisterre' in memory of Anna. This time accompanied by my eldest and youngest sisters, Sarah aged 59, Lizzie aged 47, my wife Nicky, Harry and Jake.

We had targeted the only mutually available time; the end of July 2018 to take on this new journey. A risky strategy as this would be the hottest time of the year in

Galicia with temperatures frequently rising to nearly 40 degrees.

We decided to walk with a new fundraising target of £2000, deserving financial support for the wonderful Hospice in Birmingham and honour her memory in the way it deserves.

Chapter One

Day 1: Thursday 26 July 2018
Santiago to Negreira

The Pilgrim's return

We celebrated a good team effort as we all were up and out and on the Camino de Finisterre trail by 7 am. An early start would appear to remain our best tactic over the next few days as it gets really hot in these parts by mid-afternoon.

I'm especially proud of Nicky, Lizzie and Sarah. They walked really well, they didn't moan, and they certainly did Anna's memory justice on our first day. To balance any plaudits though, I must emphasize that they were useless in the word games we created as a distraction, on the hottest tarmac trudge of the day at around 2 pm

We chatted along 'The Way' today, as we picked up the now familiar (for Jake and me at least), eucalyptus lined trails of Galicia.

Our guidebook had referenced the true pleasure that leaving the city of Santiago behind gave and I personally sensed that relief myself as we set out this morning.

Harry had been pretty nonplussed by Santiago and far from complimentary when we arrived there yesterday. He had not been with us at the end of our first Camino in 2017, so for him it was a new city. He named plenty of cities that he preferred and today I fully understood his perspective as we escaped the dry, hot and humid city into the fresher country air and lush greenery of north western Galicia.

Santiago is just a city and just a name.

Today, I realised the destinations of life don't actually matter so much, it is the learning and growing as you go and the appreciation of what you actually have that really matters. I realised too that I appreciated my new Camino family of five fellow pilgrims much more today than I did even yesterday.

What is so different between the Camino Frances trail that Jake and I walked in 2017 and the Camino de Finisterre we are walking now?

The second is less populated, there are far fewer cafés, hostels and pilgrims. Only 90% of walkers on the Camino Frances carry on to Finisterre and Muxia. Therefore, the 'Wise Pilgrim' has to be a bit more intentional about where they head for and what the hostel and food options are on the trail.

This time we are also walking as a group of six with an equal male/female mix, which could make securing six beds together in some of the smaller hostels a challenge.

This time we walk to the end of the world (as ancient pilgrims perceived Finisterre) and not to a cathedral city.

On the similarity front our pace is still good, maybe not as quick as last time, but the 3 girls are a foot shorter than Jake, Harry and I and they have a resultingly diminished stride in comparison.

Just like last time I 'think' we are all enjoying it, I'm just not going to ask Nicky till we finish!

Of course, the circumstances have one significant difference; last year we walked with a sense of thankfulness after Jake fully recovered from 2 bouts of neurosurgery in 2014 and 2016. This time we walk from a position of loss and bewilderment, as we all try to better come to terms with Anna's death last November 2017.

At one point today I mentioned to Lizzie, that I thought Anna would have really liked this Camino experience. However, I expect we might never have actually undertaken it if she was still alive, the logistics of coordinating four families who live hundreds of miles apart in the UK and France would have been far too complicated to organise. As it is, my brother Simon couldn't join us as his holiday entitlement for this year is already spent. We would have loved to have had him here with us.

For us to actually undertake this walk it took a significant incident, a tragic bereavement. My only regret today as we walked along those tree lined trails, was that Anna couldn't be here with us. We miss her.

It was a hot and sweaty afternoon; the perfect combination for a heat-influenced family squabble that can so often materialize within any group of any dynamic. For the last 5 kilometres it was truly red hot.

But everyone walked well, and everyone enjoyed each other's company. To be honest when we read of temperatures of 34 degrees in London today, we were all pretty elated that we are walking in Northern Spain in just the 28 degrees Celsius.

We got into our hostel in Negreira at 1:40 pm today. We were pretty hot but also content, satisfied and proud of our achievement.

The girls had survived their first day of the Camino experience and there was no family fall out, getting lost or blisters.

We enjoyed the Pilgrim Menu at the Imperial Bar in Negreira: 8 euros each, 48 Euros in total including a drink each. What a bargain

DISTANCE TRAVELLED: Santiago to Negreira 22 km.

Chapter Two

Day 2: Friday 27 July 2018

Negreira to Santa Marina

Nothing worthwhile is ever easy

As I lay cramped and stiff on my hostel bed this afternoon, I had an overriding sense that, every one of us (above the age of 21 at least), found today's walk much harder! So, I repeat with the emphasis of that very recent discomfort, nothing worthwhile is ever easy!

I reflected on that thought on several occasions as I walked, talked and trudged throughout today's stage and I remembered listening in recent weeks, to influential figures of national significance in the worlds of sport and politics who have spoken of how they have learned far more about themselves in the tougher situations of life than in the easy ones.

In early July 2018, I had heard Chris Froome (cyclist), Barack Obama (previous president of the USA), Bear Grylls (explorer) and most recently Gareth Southgate (manager of the England football team), all say the same thing. They had all personally developed much more when their road was rocky, than in the moments when it was all easy going and easy riding.

Of course, this whole 'little Camino' idea of ours is once again a bit nuts. Harry, Jake, Nicky and I have driven and sailed about 1700 miles over the last week just to get to Santiago so we could attempt this jaunt. Sarah has flown 1500 miles from Kent and then driven the slightly more respectable 700 miles from Toulouse with Lizzie.

All that distance and effort, before we even started walking and, now we are all lurching around like characters from a John Wayne film; bowlegged and clumsy in our feet placement, with hands best placed under our bum cheeks to aid our aching joints.

Lizzie demonstrated this beautifully as she steeled herself for the seven-metre lunge from bed to shower, she was in a state of total wipe out for the first two hours after we reached the hostel, following today's stage.

The girls may think this jaunt is crazy, but it may seem less so after meeting an elderly Dutch peregrino today, just 2 km from Santa Marina. He started walking from Eindhoven (Holland) on April 16th and will finish in Finisterre on Monday 30th July 2018. He will have walked over 2000 km in those four months. He was probably in his mid-seventies!

Good for him. That is an epic achievement and it made me think that perhaps in a couple of years I could consider something similar; maybe even starting from Halifax!

I think it is fair to claim that the achievement always feels bigger if you have to negotiate a bit of pain in order to finish what you set out to do. We felt pain today but again, there was no moaning or complaining from any in our group; a streak of steel is already visible in each of them.

Sarah and I talked about our love for Anna today as we walked, she, perhaps more than any of us, will feel Anna's absence deeply.

Sarah and Anna were always 'thick as thieves' from the outset of childhood. With only a two-year age gap, their lives were intertwined from those early years. They experienced some tough times together as they grew up which helped to forge as unique a bond of sisterhood as is possible. We both reflected as we walked. We talked about how unique and unusual Anna's length of service to the hospice had been. She had served that Community for 21 years, offering care and dignity in the long night time hours when it was most needed by the patients. Data shows patients are far more likely to die at night. Anna carried the burden and privilege of supporting hundreds of people in their final and true hour of need. This showed such an immense commitment and Anna demonstrated a level of loyalty that was definitely worthy of recognition

Tomorrow we will all trudge on, enjoy this unique experience despite the pain, seeking to share the many good times our sister, sister in law or auntie blessed us within those previous years.

DISTANCE TRAVELLED:
22 km Negreira to Santa Marina
Total walked: 44 km

Chapter Three

Day 3: Saturday 28 July 2018

Santa Marina to Logroso

Do it again, but better

Today I was reminded of the Children's game 'Boppit'.

You may know it? An American hand held, battery operated game where you were challenged to 'twist it, spin it, pull it, flick it' or 'BOPPIT.'

My children will tell you that I was useless at Boppit. That knowledge still hurts. I rarely scored higher than 20 where they would score well over 200. We took the game all over France, for several summers in a row; circa 2009. I never got past the mental stumbling block of 20, which was when the instructions started to speed up and the likelihood of my brain working faster than my hands increased.

The punch line of Boppit was: 'Do it again, but better.' That epitaph was always delivered to me way too soon, as I approached that lamentable maximum score of 20 or so.

The same tag line seems to apply to this, our second Camino in 2 years. Only this time it perhaps should read 'Do it again, but differently.'

This was an increasingly different experience for Jake and me but all the more welcome because of those differences.

This Camino we were walking shorter distances, and I'm actually quite glad we were. Harry and Jake probably thought these daily walking distances were way too easy, last year our daily average exceeded 30 km. For me I'm relishing the shorter distances, especially as my left calf is really aching. I've also been totally content to walk at a more conservative 4 km per hour as opposed to last year's 6.5 km per hour average.

Doing things, we have done before, doesn't mean we always have to do them in the same way. In fact, as I've progressed through the last few years, I've found that doing something familiar, but in a different way, can be hugely satisfying.

Today I felt quite satisfied because everyone in the group is enjoying this experience. As I reminded Nicky this afternoon; if they weren't enjoying it then we would now know about it for sure. Typically, group dynamics in more stressful circumstances, seem to fracture after approximately 48 hours. Reality TV shows like The Apprentice, I'm a celebrity or The Island would appear to demonstrate this point. Three days into our Camino, we are still not at each other's throats; just yet!

Today we settled for a shorter stage of 18.5 km. Despite Lizzie's feet hurting, all 3 of the girls professed enjoyment and satisfaction with today's walk.

We were only two days from Finisterre but planned to extend our walk by walking onto Muxia over another two days.

We are all enjoying the 'Camino Bubble' where modern distractions just don't seem to trouble you.

The hostels have been pristine though the 'International Snoring Brigade' is still alive and kicking and we have discovered that Lizzie is the International Director! Allegedly I am a founding father.

I reflected further on Anna today.

I re-remembered the time in our sleepy childhood village in Norfolk when as a six-year old I 'ran away' from the tiny village primary school because the village bully had punched me. At the time, I clearly thought that I had run away, in truth I probably ran less than 200 metres from the actual school gates and was probably only absent without leave for about 30 minutes. I was scared of him and he had hurt me, so I ran.

Anna was at the same primary school and heard about the fracas via the school grapevine. In typical Anna style she confronted the bully; five minutes later he had a split lip and a bloody nose. He never bothered me again! On leaving primary school our paths never crossed again but I do like to hope that the boy she confronted all those years ago saw the error of his ways on that day and a life improving change of attitude consequently resulted.

That was the sort of woman Anna was. She hated injustice of any kind and would never shirk away from confronting what she thought was wrong. Anna was a formidable woman. She had a definite gift for standing up for the waifs and strays and misfits of society. She told things how it was. I didn't always like to hear it from her, but I would gladly stand and take a bollocking from her right now!

We all miss her.

DISTANCE TRAVELLED:
Santa Marina to Logroso: 18.5 km
Total walked: 60.5 km

Chapter Four

Day 4: Sunday 29 July 2018

Logroso to San Roque

There is no defined way

It seems almost impossible to get lost on both the Camino Frances and Camino Finisterre.

Every 100 metres or so, you see one of the iconic blue and yellow tiles with the Camino shell engraving and directional arrow or else one of the more clumsily hand painted yellow arrows that indicate your route to Finisterre, Santiago or your next overnight stop. Unless serious weather impacted on your daily toil, you would be hard pressed to get lost on this route.

Our guidebook indicates that the normal pilgrim would take four possibly five days to walk to Finisterre and Muxia. We would appear to be on for a six-day Camino. The guidebook could suggest, but we already knew there is no definitive way to walk a Camino. We have chosen to pick our own time, route and stop offs.

In an experience of contrasts and comparisons with our Camino Frances last year, we are walking this route in a totally different way: a different pace, different route, with different perspectives and for different reasons. In just the same way in the journey of our lives I've realised there is often no defined way to do things. In life, trials and challenges will come our way, we will all face them, and we will all have to fathom a way to negotiate them.

For me I've learnt to lean on my faith more and more as it helps me to attempt to define a way through the most difficult of life's challenges. I've had my share of difficulties but have met many people who've faced much tougher times. I've also realised over the past nine months, that there is no defined way to grieve and mourn in a time of acute sorrow. I've learnt that when we suffer loss, we have to find our own way to deal with, process and ultimately progress on with it.

My sister's death had rocked me! I know my contribution to work and family life at that time was fairly rubbish; my personal input into the family Christmas was non-existent. I was fortunate enough to be carried by my fantastic wife and kids at home and some brilliant people at work.

It happened just three weeks before Christmas 2017, such a busy time in our school and family setting. I chose to deal with it by hiding in the busyness and losing myself in any attempt at normality I could find. Others in the extended family couldn't face work or normality, they had to take time out.

I've realised that no way was the defined right way of dealing with this tragic news. We all did our best and continue to try to do our best as we seek to come to terms with our loss. Was my way the right way? For me yes. But only for me.

In more recent months I've sometimes reproached myself for an inability to cry. I can't explain my lack of tears, why can't I show that level of outward emotion? However, last Wednesday when I saw my elder sister Sarah visibly upset in Santiago it made me very tearful.

It was exactly the same when I visited Anna's husband Tony. I think my deeper emotions must be triggered by the impact of loss on the people I really care about.

I guess our hope; the hope of all our family is that over time Anna's death will become less raw. This journey to Finisterre seems an appropriate staging post in that quest.

Today our group enjoyed a Sunday morning lie in. The weather is still very cloudy and as a result cooler, which is a real blessing. We could actually get some rain today.

Tonight, we stay in a donativo hostel, the only one on the Camino de Finisterre, about 14 km from the Cape. We are all excited about this hostel run by 'hospitalleros' who host and cook for the pilgrims. The donativo experience was very special last year. We expect it to be a poignant and special evening with us being so near to Finisterre.

I'm anticipating that the 'end of the world' will have an impact, particularly as we hope to witness the sunset over the lighthouse and fire pit on Monday.

Today we saw the sea for the first time.

DISTANCE TRAVELLED: Logroso to San Roque: 17 km
Total walked: 77.5 km

Chapter FIVE

Day 5: Monday 30 July 2018

San Roque to Cape Finisterre

Service above self

I've always loved and respected the culture of volunteering. One day, when I have finished working full time, I hope I will be a loyal and hard-working volunteer.

'Service above Self' is the official motto of the International Rotary movement. I've been privileged enough to witness their efforts and the efforts of other committed volunteers; like Karen, a lady who has volunteered with my Swimming class at Ravenscliffe High School for over 20 years. Volunteers underpin our work at school, helping achieve better outcomes for the students. The best volunteers are always a class act.

Last night we were fortunate enough to benefit from an example of volunteering of the highest calibre.

We were greeted, hosted and catered for by a husband and wife team named Santiago and Maria. They were lovely and oozed humility, kindness and compassion. The world would truly be a better place if more people could match their spirit of generosity. They live in San Sebastián and had driven 8 hours to San Roque specifically to host clean and cook for pilgrims. The donativo experience they provided did not disappoint. We ate a communal meal of mixed salad, chorizo and lentil soup. For the 3 Moorman Boys, 3 helpings of each was sublime.

Santiago, our host had actually walked a 3,000 km Camino in 2012, from Belgium to the bottom point of Spain. His travels were published. What a story!

We shared the donativo hostel with a Spaniard named Julio and three Czech girls from Prague and Bratislava. Like Nicky and I they were teachers in Special Education.

What a fun night.

Jake proved up to the challenge of interpreter, from Spanish to English and vice versa. We played cards; 'Cam-uno' – our own Camino derivative of the popular game 'Uno'. We chatted, ate and washed up together. The simple things in life never seemed so good, there was no isolated activity on screens. We all embraced the opportunity to just enjoy each other's company.

To me the evening summed up the true spirit of the Camino. The welcome of the hospitallero volunteers was simply amazing.

My sister Anna had that same welcoming spirit. She truly was 'the glue for our family.' She was the who checked out the welfare of the others, the one who fought our causes (sometimes literally). She cared about people, but mostly those on the margins, who were friendless or living lives in difficulty or turmoil. She was an 'old school' nurse: personal care, relational support and patient dignity were her mantras.

I remembered how she'd driven with Tony her husband, the 100+ miles to Halifax to check Jake out one Sunday afternoon soon after his second bout of surgery. No fuss or drama, she just appeared, with a pre-prepared lunch despite the fact that she was back on the night shift that same evening. I've always tried to put personal time, energy and effort into pastoral care and support for others, but Anna was a certain and consistent 2 leagues higher than any of my efforts.

Today was the start of our penultimate day of walking to Muxia. Tomorrow we walk along the coast in nice weather: it should be good.

DISTANCE TRAVELLED:
San Roque to Cape Finisterre: 17 km
Total walked: 94.5 km

Chapter Six

Day 6: Tuesday 31 July 2018

Finisterre to Lires

Time flies: no pain, no gain

Today we found the sea at Lires. The 3 boys swam, the girls chilled out and nursed their feet. The sea and beach were fantastic. Unbelievably, this time last week, we had just started to walk the Camino Finisterre.

I remember us setting off clearly; walking through the still dark streets of Santiago whilst most of the city slept. There had been a nervous apprehension on that morning, more especially I guess amongst the 3 girls as they really were unsure as to what they were letting themselves into.

Tomorrow when they arrive in Muxia on our 7th day of this Camino, I think there will be a fair degree of satisfaction that they have actually made it. We carry a few scars of the last week between us. 'No pain no gain' may be a bit of a cliché, but I feel it does readily apply in this context.

Harry, Liz and I have 'Camino Toe.' Basically, our big toe nails have started to blacken, and I suspect will eventually fall off! On the steep downhill stretches of the Camino, (there are a lot of them) your feet often slip forward inside your shoes and giving your big toe a battering as a result. It hurts.

Nicky and Sarah both sport blisters. Nicky ended up walking in sandals today and had a slight limp as she entered Lires. She resisted the beach detour, it was a step too far; another 1 kilometre walk each way and her feet were just too painful. She chilled in a hammock at the hostel and enjoyed some down time.

Jake has now started a course of antibiotics for an infection he picked up before we even set off. All 3 boys all have a number of very itchy mosquito bites.

So, once again the Camino has taken a bit of toll on all of us and I think we are all quite tired. Don't forget, the hostel snorers take an additional toll every night.

The night before we'd set out from Santiago we had sat out in a courtyard as the sun was setting and had pondered what a pilgrimage meant to each one of us. All six of us gave answers that perhaps cumulatively grabbed the essence of 'The Camino'. They included: testing, a spiritual perspective, a sense of history as we tread in the footsteps of the thousands who have walked this route before us, a time for reflection, an element of sacrifice, an opportunity to de- clutter the mind and to meet like-minded others from different countries and cultures, a chance to reduce to the bare essentials what we choose to carry every day, a chance to walk for our sister. Plus, a likelihood of some pain and discomfort.

Doing a Camino hurts. It always carries a cost, but at the same time it really does liberate and rejuvenate.

I suspect that Nicky won't do a Camino again. It's not her thing. She did this Camino and finished it, not particularly because she wanted to walk it, but because she wanted to support us to walk it. She should be very proud.

Liz had to grind it out at times. I think she found it quite tough and I think the persistent walking definitely hurt her at times, but she is no quitter and was never going to fail to complete this walk.

Sarah seemed to cope very well especially as the oldest -peregrino of our group! Sarah is no stranger to hiking but she too definitely found this a challenge. She may possibly undertake a Camino again, I think her husband Steve might be up for it, but probably on a bike. Remember to take a bell if you do Steve.

Jake and Harry breezed it. For them it was probably way too easy, but it was lovely how they adapted their pace to match the walking speed of the slowest walkers in the group. Their incessant banter was a boost in the times where it all got a bit emotional or physically hard.

At the heart of everything, and leaving all of the above to one side, we walked this Camino in memory of a sister, sister in law and Auntie, who we loved and miss. Hopefully it has been a help and cathartic? There were conversations, tears, confusion Why? How? I guess these emotions are natural consequences of loss. The pain doesn't go away. Maybe it diminishes over time.

There was laughter, memories of fun times and an appreciation of the time we had shared together.

The loss of Anna brought us together to do something special. With one day to go there are no regrets, except that she wasn't here physically to do it with us. Her spirit was here though I'm sure.

We have almost finished.

It is 7.30 pm on Thursday 2 August 2018 and we have completed our challenge. A walk that the guidebooks suggested could be completed in 4 days took us 6 and a bit. Who cares? We did it the way we wanted, and I think it was all the better because we did so.

We split the last and extra 27 km to Muxia into a walk of 2 sections and spent our final hostel experience in Lires. We enjoyed more of the 'Spirit of the Camino' with a meal with an Israeli couple called Val and Ophra and Julio from Spain, who we had met at San Roque. It was great fun, not least because of the language barrier, even though Julio spoke no English and most of us could speak very little Spanish. There was no barrier. We all made ourselves understood even when we didn't have the words. Jake translated most of what we said into Spanish when we couldn't express ourselves.

I was reminded of the real joy we can all experience when we eat together, even within the hustle and bustle of fast living 21st century life, that so often prevents us performing that very simple daily act. If I could protect just one thing for the future, it would be to ensure that my family and friends continue to eat together on a daily basis. It has been at the core of school life at Ravenscliffe, lunch remains a communal act each and every day. It was part of my childhood and has been an unconditional part of our family life for our 29 years of marriage. Many of our best times, my best times have been around the meal table.

DISTANCE TRAVELLED:
Finisterre to Lires 14 km
Total walked: 108.5 km

Chapter Seven

Day 7: Wednesday 1 August 2018

Lires to Muxia

Back to life, back to reality

We finished walking today one week after starting out.

The walk from Lires to Muxia was quite pretty and apart from one steep climb, reasonably gentle. We messed around with a second Survival Skills 'Camino style' film, making fire from sand on a beach just outside Muxia. Very silly but who cares?

We rolled into Muxia at 1:30 pm and headed out to the chapel next to the sea, which had been used as the final scene in the Hollywood film 'The Way.' The film that had first inspired Jake and I to tackle the Camino Frances last year in 2017.

We caught the afternoon bus back to Santiago and stayed overnight in the same Airbnb that we had left a week before at the outset of our walk.

Have we learned anything in the last week?

Yes, a lot. Nothing deeply profound perhaps: just a greater understanding that people matter. It is okay to grieve in a way that suits you and your personality and that in the journey of life we will all have tough times and that these can at least be eased by the people we choose to surround ourselves with.

Our Fellowship has now broken, and we have all now left Santiago to go back to our lives. We had a blast, even though it was tough walking at times.

I felt this walk was a fitting way to mark my sister's legacy.

I suspect I will return for another Camino. When? Who knows?

DISTANCE TRAVELLED: Lires to Muxia: 14 km
Total walked: 122.5 km

Chapter Eight

Thursday 2nd August 2018

Concluding thoughts: The road goes on....

We attended the Pilgrim Mass in Santiago Cathedral at noon today, though this time they didn't swing the huge botafumeiro incense burner that hangs from the ceiling of the church.

The heat had returned, and it was blisteringly hot in Santiago 38 degrees when we left at 2:30 pm. We had been blessed by fantastic walking weather in our seven-day hike, whilst the rest of Europe sizzled in a heatwave. The forecast for the next few days predicted even hotter weather and we realized that we were so fortunate in our week of walking. It never got hotter than 28 degrees and most of the time we walked in temperatures of 18-23 Celsius which was perfect. We were definitely blessed. I'm don't think we could have walked it in the extreme heat.

Sarah and Lizzie drove east this afternoon planning to stop off overnight in a hotel (no longer true Pilgrims) in the Picos mountains near Santander.

Nicky, Jake, Harry and I drove 2 hours south to a campsite overlooking the Atlantic west of Vigo. Harry will fly from Vigo to Edinburgh on Saturday, Jake from Porto to Manchester on Saturday too. The 'Dad Taxi Service' will be back in full operational mode by next Saturday morning.

Nicky and I planned on chilling (sweating is currently more likely) in northern Portugal, Spain and France, for the next 2 weeks. I think we are all glad we did this challenge.

Our walking company had now splintered, but we had all shared a unique experience. Our Camino adventures have ended, for now at least.

I sincerely hope our simple walking efforts have achieved our targets of celebrating Jake's recovery and honouring the memory of my sister Anna.

Has the Camino de Finisterre helped us as we mourn her loss?

Maybe, maybe not.

It is always going to be a very personal perspective as to whether something like this actually helps. For me it was good to talk and walk. It is always good to talk and walk.

Even as I moved from the conclusion of the Camino to the enjoyment of a three-week holiday with my family in northern Spain, I could still feel the strong pull of the Camino.

The final irony perhaps lies in the location of our first 2 campsites after our Camino.

At the start of August, we camped right next to a Camino route, near Baiona on the Spanish/Portuguese boarder. The Portuguese Camino from Lisbon to Santiago was literally just 25 metres away from the front zip of my tent. It follows the coast and is 260 miles long.

It was hugely Ironic that one week later on our second camp site 40 km west of Santander on the northern coast of Spain we found ourselves once again, less than 50 metres from the 'Camino del Norte.' It is an 830 km Camino that follows the coast of northern Spain. It starts in Irun in the French Pyrenees. Once again it looks a fantastic walk.

The pull for me to walk both of those paths was strong.

I suspect I will be back. Maybe I will cycle a future Camino, with a bell of course! The third option to guarantee a Compostela in Santiago, is to ride on horseback. Rest assured, that won't be happening.

I've learned in life and in the last four years in particular, that nothing is really for certain. Both of my Camino efforts have been fuelled by challenging personal circumstances.

What challenges will I have to face in the future? I know not and perhaps it is best that I don't know. All I know is that the Camino of my life continues, and I must try to live it in the best way I can.

The words of JRR Tolkien in 'The Lord of the Rings' are as good a place as any to finish this very personal story about the Camino's recent influence on my life.

The Road goes ever on and on,
Down from the door where it began.
Now far ahead the Road has gone,
And I must follow if I can,
Pursuing it with wary feet,
Until it joins some larger way,
Where many paths and errands meet.
And whither then? I cannot say.

Martin Moorman

31st December 2018

The Author

Martin Moorman was 54 years of age when he wrote this book. Happily married for 29 years, Martin and his wife Nicky have 3 grown up children, Rosie, Harry and Jake.

Martin is the Headteacher of Ravenscliffe High School in Halifax, a generic special school for students aged 11-19 who all have learning difficulties.

In his spare time, he likes to spend time with his immediate and extended family, taking photographs and going walking. Since 2014, trudging along Caminos has become one of his favourite pastimes.

15 year old schoolboy Jake Moorman was a
typical teenager, loving life, his skateboard and
only doing his school work when he had to. In
2014 his life dramatically changed when a serious
brain haemorrhage meant he had to consent to
complex neurosurgery 'or die on the ward.'
Written by his dad Martin, Jake's story connects
with the unique nature of the historic 500 mile
Camino de Santiago in northern Spain. It bears
testimony to a teenager's incredible courage and
faith and to the alluring power of hope within the
most desperate of circumstances.

ISBN: 978-3-7103-3582-2

9 783710 335822